The New CAST IRON Cookbook

MORE THAN 200 RECIPES for TODAY'S KITCHEN

Adams Media

Adams media

AVON, MASSACHUSETTS

W9-BEI-886

Copyright © 2015 by F+W Media, Inc.
All rights reserved.
This book, or parts thereof, may not be reproduced in any form without permission from the publisher; exceptions are made for brief excerpts used in published reviews.

Published by
Adams Media, a division of F+W Media, Inc.
57 Littlefield Street, Avon, MA 02322. U.S.A.
www.adamsmedia.com

Contains material adapted from *The Everything® Cast-Iron Cookbook* by Cinnamon Cooper, copyright © 2010 by F+W Media, Inc., ISBN 10: 1-4405-0225-0, ISBN 13: 978-1-4405-0225-5.

ISBN 10: 1-4405-8976-3
ISBN 13: 978-1-4405-8976-8
eISBN 10: 1-4405-8977-1
eISBN 13: 978-1-4405-8977-5

Printed in the United States of America.

10   9   8   7   6   5   4   3   2

Library of Congress Cataloging-in-Publication Data

The new cast-iron cookbook / Adams Media.
    pages cm
  Includes index.
  ISBN 978-1-4405-8976-8 (pb) -- ISBN 1-4405-8976-3 (pb)
-- ISBN 978-1-4405-8977-5 (ebook) -- ISBN 1-4405-8977-1
(ebook)
  1. Skillet cooking. 2. Cast-iron. I. Adams Media (Firm)
  TX840.S55N49 2015
  641.7'7--dc23
                              2015015385

Cover design by Frank Rivera.
Cover images © iStockphoto.com/Fisechko_Anastasia.
Interior photos © ziashusha/123RF, StockFood/Bill, Arce, and iStockphoto.com/Natalia Van Doninck/Lauri Patterson/martinturzak/space-monkey-pics/Lcc54613/zi3000/john shepherd/cheche22/jandara/fotostreet/haoliang/KathyDewar/SouthernLightStudios/jjpoole/sf_foodphoto/lorenzoantonucci/LynnSeeden/Studio_Tartaglione/nicolesy/mushakesa/Syldavia/Renphoto/kdow/tbralnina/boblin/gbh007/wsmahar/Zoryanchik/Paul_Brighton/haha21/tycoon751/minadezhda/Alexcrab/Tsuji.

This book is available at quantity discounts for bulk purchases. For information, please call 1-800-289-0963.

Contents

Introduction

Skillets. Griddles. Dutch ovens.

If you thought cast iron was old news, think again! Today, this durable cookware is making a comeback and, with *The New Cast-Iron Cookbook*, you'll find yourself impressing your guests with delicious meals in no time.

Throughout the book, you'll find more than 200 modern, mouthwatering dishes that are perfect for all occasions. From breakfast and brunch to appetizers and entrées to sweets and desserts, you'll learn how to cook anything you can imagine in the world's most indestructible pots and pans. And, whether you're an experienced cast-iron cooker or have never picked up a skillet in your life, you'll soon find yourself whipping up dishes like Fresh Fig Muffins, Swiss Chard and Lentil Soup, Miso-Glazed Salmon, and more with confidence and ease.

You may also be wondering how you should go about choosing a cast-iron pan in the first place. Can you restore the vintage one you found at the antique store up the street, or should you buy something new? How do you season cast-iron cookware? And, once you've cooked with these pots and pans, how do you get them clean? All these questions and more will be answered in Chapter 1, which tells you everything you need to know about the recently revived art of cast-iron cooking.

So, grab your cast-iron pots and pans and get ready to make the old new again.

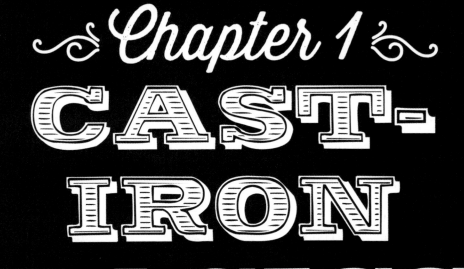

Chapter 1
CAST-IRON

BASICS

You know you want to cook with cast iron, but you know there's special care involved. You've heard that you have to season it and clean it differently than you do other cookware, but how? In this chapter, you'll learn everything you need to know about how to choose and care for your cast-iron pan, the benefits of cooking with cast iron, and more!

Why Cook with Cast Iron?

You know cast iron is on-trend, but why? What exactly is it about these heavy pots and pans that makes them a perennial favorite for everyone who's serious about great food? Well, cast-iron cooking doesn't just bring great taste. It also brings an array of benefits—some of which may not even have crossed your mind. Let's take a look and learn what cast iron can do for you.

LOW COST, HIGH VALUE

If you think cast-iron pots and pans are outrageously expensive, think again! New cast-iron skillets actually cost 10–50 percent less than skillets made from other materials. For just $15–$20 for new skillets, you'll come home with a pan that will gain value with each dish you make. And, if you buy and restore those vintage pots and pans that you find at a yard sale, flea market, or estate sale, or if you inherit cast-iron cookware from someone else in your family, even that small investment can go down considerably. And, no matter what you spend (or don't spend) on your cast-iron dishes, they're guaranteed to last a lifetime—or longer—so you're sure to get your money's worth!

IT CAN BE USED OVER HIGH HEAT

Many nonstick and other lightweight pans cannot be used over high heat. Because the metal is thin and conducts heat quickly, they can get too hot and then cool off easily. But, since most cast-iron pans are manufactured from a single, solid piece of metal, you can begin the cooking process on the stovetop and finish in the oven or under a broiler, and you can even place your cast-iron cookware directly over the hot coals on a grill or over a campfire. Make sure you know your pan, though. Some enameled pans come with a tempered plastic handle, and some Dutch ovens have metal handles that won't be able to handle extreme heat.

CAST IRON PROVIDES EVEN HEAT

This thick, dense metal that we discussed in the previous section absorbs and conducts heat slowly and evenly. Although a cast-iron pan takes longer to get hot after placing it on a burner, it's more likely to stay hot when you add cold foods. The even heating also makes it great for cooking sauces or things that may burn easily. If the pan is made properly, it will keep almost the same temperature on the edges as it does in the center. And since cast iron retains heat so well, you'll find that it makes a great serving vessel.

When cooking with cast iron, always preheat your pan if you're going to be cooking on the stove or want a crispy crust on something you're baking in the oven. This preheating step takes a few more minutes, but gives much better results.

CAST IRON PROMOTES CRISPING

Not everything that comes out of a cast-iron pan is going to be crispy, but if you're cooking something that should have a crispy or even crunchy exterior and a soft interior, cast iron is the best choice. The surface of the pan encourages food to brown and crisp better than even the most expensive nonstick skillet on the market. Even a brand-new, freshly seasoned skillet can give food a crispy texture.

IT WILL BECOME A NONSTICK PAN

When you first get your cast-iron cookware, you have to season it a few times before you can cook something without worrying about it sticking. But, once you have a healthy seasoning base on your cookware, which you'll learn how to develop later in this chapter, you'll find yourself cooking with less oil than you would in other pans. When you have a skillet with at least several months of seasoning, you can cut the oil called for in the recipe by a third to a half, and you won't have to worry about scraping stuck-on food off your pan after the fact.

Cast iron's nonstick qualities give you more than just less food to scrape off your cookware,

though. Most nonstick pans are coated in Teflon, a synthetic resin that has been shown to emit fumes that are dangerous to small birds when used over high heat. So even if you're lucky enough to have a typical nonstick pan that won't warp over high heat, it may release fumes that could be toxic to your family. Cast iron doesn't give off any fumes and it imparts iron into the food cooked in it, even after it is seasoned. If you tend to be anemic, you may be able to reduce your supplement intake by cooking most of your dishes in cast iron. Be sure to follow your doctor's orders and get tested before changing your prescribed health plan.

A SEASONED SKILLET LEADS TO HEALTHIER COOKING

Cook dishes with a high fat or oil content the first eight to ten times you use a new cast-iron skillet. As your skillet gets more seasoned, you'll need less fat and oil. And because the surface and metal used in your skillet will help you create a crust on foods, you won't miss that fat. With cast iron, even your boneless, skinless chicken breasts will look like rustic, browned comfort food.

What Do You Need?

Before you start cooking with cast iron, take some time to think about what you need. To start, what kind of cast-iron pan do you actually need to buy? You're probably familiar with and may even own a cast-iron skillet, but a skillet isn't the only pot or pan available. As you look to buy either new or vintage cast iron, consider investing in the following pots and pans, all of which are used to create the delicious cast-iron recipes found throughout the book:

- Chicken fryer
- Corn stick pan
- Dutch oven
- Griddle
- Grill pan
- Muffin pan
- Skillet
- And so many more!

In addition to this variety, when it comes to cast iron, you can choose pots and pans that are:

- New
- Used
- Enameled
- Nonenameled
- Unseasoned
- Pre-seasoned

Used pans are likely to come from a yard sale, flea market, online auction, or as a gift. Enameled pans are cast-iron pans that have a glass, enameled coating, usually on the inside and out. This coating is often white on the inside and comes in a variety of colors on the outside, depending on the manufacturer.

All of these options have differences that you should keep in mind while purchasing.

BRAND-NEW CAST-IRON COOKWARE

When buying new cookware, look for pans that don't have any large pits, bumps, or cracks on the cooking surface. These imperfections can make it harder to cook with your pan. Ideally the pan will be dull gray and have a texture similar to that of a piece of high-grit sandpaper. As you cook with it, it will become blacker and smoother. You also want to make sure that the thickness of the bottom and sides of the pan is even. Pans with bottoms and sides that get thinner around the edge are less likely to conduct heat evenly and are more likely to break.

VINTAGE CAST-IRON COOKWARE

Cast-iron pans, if cared for properly, get better with age because they become more seasoned each time they're used. Even an old pan that is rusted or covered in bumpy residue can be salvaged, and will likely be better than a new one.

Before you buy a vintage cast-iron pan, take a close look at the merchandise. Make sure your pan doesn't have cracks, even if they don't go all the way through. Look for black epoxy used to fill any pits or cracks. It can be hard to see epoxy-filled cracks, but if you see black paint, ask before you buy if you intend to cook with it.

Epoxy is poisonous and will release toxins when heated.

How to Season (or Reseason) a Pan

The interior of a new pan has a roughly textured surface, but a fully seasoned skillet is smooth and black. Every time you use the cast-iron pot or pan, as long as you clean it properly (discussed later in this chapter), you season the pan or bond the oils and fats from the cooking process into its surface.

Note, however, that if you have a pan with an enameled coating on the inside, the enameling process eliminates the need for seasoning. With a quick wash, these dishes are ready to use straight out of the box. Because they can't be seasoned, you may find yourself using more oil than a recipe calls for, but because the iron isn't in touch with the food, you don't have to worry about cooking dishes high in acid in a new skillet.

SEASONING THE UNSEASONED PAN

When you buy a cast-iron pan at the store, you'll notice that it will be covered in a paraffin-like or shellac coating, which the manufacturer places on the pan to protect its surface. Before you go any further in the seasoning process, you will need to remove this coating by washing and scrubbing the pan in hot, soapy water. Be sure to clean every edge, the handle, and the outside of the skillet thoroughly. Dry it completely before proceeding. Then, fill the skillet with water, place it over a medium burner, and let the water evaporate. If you smell a strong chemical smell, wash and dry the skillet again.

Now that your pan is clean, it's time to add the first seasoning layer. Preheat the oven to 350°F and place a layer of aluminum foil or a baking sheet on the bottom rack of the oven. Then, take a tablespoon-sized chunk of shortening and rub it over the entire interior and exterior surface of the skillet; any excess will drip off the pan as it bakes. Place the pan upside down in the oven and let it bake for one hour.

Once the hour is up, turn off the heat and leave the pan in the oven to cool overnight. The surface should be darker, but it won't be black and shiny yet. It will take several uses and proper cleaning to get the desired appearance.

Note that during the seasoning process, you'll likely notice a slight burning smell and see some smoke. This is normal and should not be a cause for concern. During this process, the oil you applied to the pan smokes, and the pan soaks up both the oil and the carbonization that it creates.

CLEANING AND PREPPING THE PRE-SEASONED PAN

If you're not quite ready for the time commitment that an unseasoned, cast-iron pan needs, you can buy pre-seasoned pieces at the store. Before using one of these pots or pans, you just need to wash it with hot water (no soap!) and a stiff-bristled brush. Dry the pan completely, pour some vegetable oil on a paper towel, and rub it over the surface of the pan until you're ready to use it.

There is some disagreement about whether pre-seasoned skillets are worth their greater cost. This cookware is typically more expensive, and some say that the factory-applied seasoning doesn't hold up as well as the seasoning that you could apply at home. However, if you only plan on using your cast-iron pan occasionally, not having to go through the steps previously described for an unseasoned skillet may make the higher price worth it.

PREPPING A HEALTHY OLDER SKILLET

Some vintage cast-iron cookware will come to you in fantastic shape—and some won't. If you've bought or inherited the former, your path to the oven will be an easy one. If the inside of the skillet is smooth and shiny, all you need to do is rinse it with hot water, dry it thoroughly, and wipe it with a fresh coating of oil. If you're concerned about latent bacteria, place an inch of water in the pan and put it over high heat. Let the water boil for one minute. Hold the pan over a sink and swirl the pan around so the hot water coats the interior. Then simply dry it and coat it with oil before using.

PREPPING A NEEDY OLDER SKILLET

If you have a vintage cast-iron pan that's in rusty, dirty, or otherwise rough shape, you have to restore it to its former glory before you'll be ready to cook. To start, you need to sand off rust with steel wool, large-grit sandpaper, a rust eraser, a small steel brush, or even just scouring powder. Thick, carbonized residue can be removed by placing your skillet in the oven during the self-cleaning cycle. You can also spray the pan with oven cleaner, place it in a plastic bag, and let it sit for a few days. Wash the pan thoroughly using soap and water and scrub the affected areas with steel wool if necessary to get back to the bare metal.

After you've stripped the rust or corrosion off the pan, you'll need to follow the same seasoning steps as you would for a new pan. If the pan seems dry and isn't glossy after the initial seasoning, it may mean the oil used in the seasoning has soaked into the surface of the pan. If this is the case, pour some vegetable oil on a paper towel and rub it over the entire surface of the pan. Place the pan over medium heat and let it cook until the oil starts to smoke. Turn off the heat and let the pan cool to the touch before using.

How to Clean Cast Iron

Unless you're hanging your newly seasoned cast-iron pan for decoration, you're going to need to care for it slightly differently than you would your other cookware. Because it must be maintained differently, cast iron scares away many people, but if cared for correctly, you'll find cleanup time is actually faster than with other pots and pans. The main rule of cleaning a cast-iron pan is avoid using soap on it once it's been seasoned. Using soap won't ruin it, but it will remove some of the seasoning that you've worked to build up.

Make sure your pan is hot before you try to clean it. A hot pan is easier to clean than a cold skillet because the metal is expanded and more likely to release what is stuck to it. Pour in ½ tablespoon of water and a tablespoon of kosher salt. Wad up a paper towel, hold it with tongs, and rub it over the surface of the pan to loosen anything stuck to it. (The salt will help grind away debris.) When the salt looks dirty, dump it out, wipe the surface clean, and your pan is sealed and ready for storage.

If you have a particularly stubborn mess or if your paper towel starts to fall apart, pour 2 table-spoons of salt (kosher or pickling salt works best) in the skillet and cut a potato in half. Hold the potato like a scrub brush and rub it firmly over the surface of the skillet. The salt should act like scouring powder to help you rub off the stuck-on food. Neither the potato nor the salt will damage the surface of the pan, and the potato will protect your fingertips from abrasions.

If you still can't remove the mess, which is more likely to happen with a new skillet, try scraping it with a butter knife. This may result in spots that are lighter than the rest of the pan, but these will disappear after a few uses. And if nothing else seems to help, use some hot and soapy water. This should be a last resort since it does remove some of the seasoning.

CLEANING ENAMELED CAST IRON

Cleaning enameled cast-iron pans is relatively easy. You should simply wash them with hot, soapy water. Because the enameled surface can scratch, you should use only plastic scrub-brushes and sponges. Note that the lighter-colored surfaces can stain fairly easy, but soaking them for a few hours in a mild bleach solution will remove the stains. Also, keep in mind that day-to-day care for enameled cast-iron cookware is trickier than nonenameled cookware. Because the enameling can scratch, be sure to use only wooden, plastic, nylon, or silicone cooking tools.

How to Store Your Cast-Iron Pans

Since the majority of cast-iron pans don't scratch, you can stack them together. You can also hang them from a firmly attached pot rack, or leave them on the stovetop or in the oven, like many cast-iron users do. If you rarely cook or if you have to store your pans for an extended period of time, it's best to coat them lightly in vegetable oil inside and out. You also want to oil newer pans after each use, and you especially want to oil pans that you've had to clean with soapy water. The oil not only keeps the pan from rusting, it also keeps the oil that's already on the rough surface of the pan from drying up. In addition, as time goes on, this also makes the pan easier to clean and cook with.

The surfaces of enameled cast-iron pots and pans are prone to chipping, so avoid stacking your enameled cookware when you store it. Dropping the pans can also result in chips and cracks, as can using the pans over very high heat. Because high heat can damage the enameling, it's safest to not use these pans on a grill, over a campfire, or when cooking over high heat on a stovetop.

Precautions for Cast-Iron Pans

Even though you may find yourself wanting to use your cast-iron pans for everything, there are a few things to keep in mind before you dive in to cast-iron cooking:

1. Cast iron is heavy and you'll most likely need two hands to pour from a skillet or to lift a full pan out of the oven.
2. Highly acidic foods can often end up tasting metallic if cooked in a less-than-seasoned pan. The acid can also cause a pan's seasoning to dissolve. Make sure to use an enameled or a well-seasoned pan when you're cooking with tomatoes or tomato sauce, wine, beer, citrus juices, or vinegars.
3. The recipes in this book provide cooking times for cast-iron pans. Because of the even-heating properties of cast-iron pans, when you're using other recipes for different types of cookware, you may find that you need to reduce cooking times by 5–10 percent.
4. Serving food in cast iron makes a great presentation and keeps the food warmer longer than if you transfer it to a bowl. But never store food in your skillet in the refrigerator or on a table for more than a few hours. The acids and liquids in the foods will start to break down the seasoning. Once the seasoning starts to break down, your food will begin to taste metallic. There is nothing carcinogenic or poisonous about this taste, but many people find it off-putting.
5. Hot liquids can also remove the seasoning from pans if you're not careful. If you've only used your Dutch oven a few times, boiling liquids may cause the seasoning to start to dissolve along the edges. If you notice that your seasoning is worse after cooking, wash the skillet normally, then dry it by placing it over medium heat on your stovetop and rubbing some oil into the surface of the pan while it is hot. As the pan cools it will absorb the oil and will be ready for your next use.
6. If you have a glass top range, don't drag the pans across the range. This will scratch the

surface. Because it takes a while for electric ranges to cool down, move your cast-iron pan off the burner if you want it to stop cooking. Alternately, if you're close to finishing a dish, you can turn off the burner but leave the pan in place so it finishes cooking slowly.

7. You can ruin a cast-iron pan beyond repair by changing the temperature of the skillet dramatically and quickly. If you pour ice water into a heated pan, or if you have a pan in the freezer and then place it over high heat, your cast-iron pan may crack.

Now that you know the basics on how to choose a pan, how to season it, how to cook with it, and how to clean and store it, it's time to begin cooking. So grab your cast-iron pots and pans and get ready to impress!

Chapter 2

BREAK-FAST AND BRUNCH

Blue Cheese Buttermilk Biscuits

1. Preheat oven to 350°F and place griddle in the middle of the oven.

2. Whisk the dry ingredients together in a large bowl. Cut the shortening into the dry ingredients. Stir in the blue cheese and scallions.

3. Make a well in the center and pour in 1⅓ cups of buttermilk. Fold to combine. Divide the dough into twelve even balls and drop them on the hot griddle or skillet. Brush the surface of the biscuits with 1 tablespoon of buttermilk. Bake in the center of the oven for 20–25 minutes, or until they're golden brown. Serve with butter while warm.

2½ CUPS CAKE FLOUR OR ALL-PURPOSE FLOUR

2 TEASPOONS BAKING POWDER

¾ TEASPOON KOSHER SALT

½ TEASPOON BAKING SODA

⅔ CUP CHILLED VEGETABLE SHORTENING, CUT INTO CUBES

1 CUP BLUE CHEESE, CRUMBLED

1 SCALLION, MINCED

1⅓ CUPS PLUS 1 TABLESPOON BUTTERMILK

Cornmeal Johnnycakes

1. Stir the dry ingredients in a bowl and whisk in the boiling water.

2. Place a griddle over medium-high heat. Once it's heated, add 2 tablespoons of the vegetable oil.

3. Drop the mixture onto the pan a few tablespoons at a time. Cook for 5 minutes before flipping and cooking the other side. Place them on a warmed plate until ready to serve with butter, maple syrup, or hot sauce.

1 CUP CORNMEAL

1 TEASPOON SALT

1 TEASPOON SUGAR

1½ CUPS BOILING WATER

¼ CUP VEGETABLE OIL OR BACON DRIPPINGS

ZUCCHINI PANCAKES

Zucchini Pancakes

YIELDS 24–30 PANCAKES

1. Place the zucchini in a colander. Sprinkle with 1 teaspoon salt and toss to coat evenly. Let this sit in your sink for half an hour to 1 hour if it is humid.

2. Preheat oven to 200°F so you can keep cooked pancakes warm before serving.

3. Squeeze as much of the water out of the zucchini as you can. Place them in a bowl. Sprinkle the onion over the zucchini and mix in the egg and bread crumbs.

4. Place a skillet over medium-high heat and add the oil. If it starts to smoke, lower the temperature. Use your hands to scoop up a heaping tablespoon of the mixture and flatten it into a pancake. Place it in the skillet and fry 2–3 at a time. Cook on each side for about 3 minutes until they're light brown.

5. Remove them from the skillet and place on a rack over a cookie sheet in the middle of the oven. Sprinkle with salt and pepper. Repeat with the remaining mixture until they're all cooked. Serve while warm.

1½ POUNDS ZUCCHINI (3 LARGE ZUCCHINI), SHREDDED

1 TEASPOON PLUS 1 PINCH SALT

¼ VIDALIA ONION, THINLY SLICED AND SEPARATED

1 LARGE EGG

¾ CUP FINE BREAD CRUMBS

½ CUP VEGETABLE OIL

PINCH PEPPER

SWEET POTATO LATKES

Sweet Potato Latkes

YIELDS 4-6 SERVINGS

1. Stir together the flour, sugars, baking powder, and spices in a large bowl. Whisk together the eggs and milk in a smaller bowl. Pour the egg mixture into the dry ingredients. Stir till it is barely combined. Add the grated sweet potatoes to the mix and stir till evenly coated.

2. Place a skillet over medium heat. Once it is heated, add ¼ cup of the oil to the skillet.

3. Once the oil has come to temperature, drop the potato mixture into the hot oil by the tablespoonful and flatten slightly. Cook for 2 minutes on each side.

4. Place latkes on a wire rack over paper towels and let them drain. Sprinkle them while they're hot with a dash of salt.

1 CUP FLOUR

4 TEASPOONS SUGAR

2 TEASPOONS BROWN SUGAR

2 TEASPOONS BAKING POWDER

½ TEASPOON CAYENNE POWDER

4 TEASPOONS CURRY POWDER

2 TEASPOONS GROUND CUMIN

1 TEASPOON PLUS 1 DASH SALT

¼ TEASPOON GROUND BLACK PEPPER

4 EGGS, BEATEN

½ CUP MILK

2 POUNDS SWEET POTATOES, PEELED, TRIMMED, AND GRATED

½ CUP VEGETABLE OIL

Stuffed Vienna Bread French Toast

YIELDS 4 SERVINGS

1. Cut the ends off the bread to get a rectangular loaf. Cut four 1½"-thick slices from the bread. Cut the ends in half. Take a skinny knife and cut a pocket into the bread.

2. In a small bowl, mix the cream cheese, honey, and salt. Use a knife to spread one-quarter of the cream cheese in each bread pocket. Place several strawberry pieces in each pocket. Take one of the chunks cut from the end of the loaf and wedge it into the pocket opening.

3. Place a griddle over medium heat; once it's heated, melt the butter evenly across the surface of the griddle.

4. Carefully dunk each slice of bread into the egg, making sure all of the bread is coated. Carefully place the cut end of the bread on the griddle and cook for 2 minutes before laying the bread on its side. This seals the opening to prevent the cheese from leaking out. Repeat with each slice, cooking the bread for 3–4 minutes on each side until golden brown. Serve immediately.

1 LOAF VIENNA BREAD

6 OUNCES CREAM CHEESE

2 TABLESPOONS HONEY

¼ TEASPOON SALT

1 PINT STRAWBERRIES, STEMMED AND SLICED

1 TABLESPOON BUTTER

4 EGGS, BEATEN WELL

STUFFED VIENNA BREAD FRENCH TOAST

Oatmeal and Buttermilk Muffins

YIELDS 12–18 MUFFINS

1. Place the oats and the buttermilk in a covered bowl and refrigerate for 6–24 hours. Preheat oven to 400°F. Stir the sugar, eggs, and 2 tablespoons of shortening into the oat mixture. Combine the flour, baking soda, and salt, and then fold into the oat mixture.

2. Use the remaining shortening to thoroughly grease each muffin pan cup. Fill the cups two-thirds full with batter. Bake for 20–25 minutes, until an inserted toothpick comes out clean.

3. Once the muffins are cooked through, turn them out of the pan immediately and let cool slightly before serving.

2 CUPS ROLLED OATS

1½ CUPS BUTTERMILK

½ CUP SUGAR

2 LARGE EGGS

4 TABLESPOONS SHORTENING OR BUTTER, CUT INTO SMALL CUBES

1 CUP ALL-PURPOSE FLOUR

1 TEASPOON BAKING SODA

½ TEASPOON SALT

Bacon and Sauerkraut Pancakes

YIELDS 4 MEDIUM-SIZED PANCAKES

1. Place the sauerkraut in a small strainer and let it sit over a bowl for 30 minutes. Squeeze it regularly to remove as much of the moisture as possible. Combine the flours in a medium bowl. Slowly stir in the water until it is thoroughly mixed. Add the drained sauerkraut, potato, onion, and bacon to the batter. Stir until it is combined.

2. Place a griddle over medium-high heat. Add half of the oil to the pan and swirl so it is evenly coated.

3. Pour one-quarter of the batter slowly onto the griddle. Cook for 3 minutes, or until the bottom is golden and bubbles have risen to the top. Flip it over, press against the pancake with the back of your spatula, and cook for 3 minutes. Press firmly. If batter comes through on the top, flip and cook for 1 minute before pressing to make sure the center is cooked. Repeat with the rest of the batter.

4. Transfer to a serving platter and serve with mustard.

1 CUP SAUERKRAUT

1¼ CUPS ALL-PURPOSE FLOUR

⅓ CUP RICE FLOUR

1½ CUPS WATER

1 SMALL POTATO, PEELED AND SHREDDED

1 SMALL ONION, SKINNED AND SHREDDED

4 SLICES COOKED BACON, CRUMBLED

3 TABLESPOONS VEGETABLE OIL

½ CUP MUSTARD

FRESH FIG MUFFINS

Fresh Fig Muffins

YIELDS 12 MUFFINS

1. Preheat oven 350°F. Remove the stems and cut the figs into ¼" slices and then into ¼" cubes. Place them in a small bowl and add the sherry. Let sit for about 15 minutes.

2. In a medium-sized bowl, combine the flour, almonds, salt, baking soda, cinnamon, and nutmeg. In a separate and larger mixing bowl, beat the sugar, oil, and eggs. Reduce the mixer speed to low and slowly add the flour mixture.

3. Fold the figs and sherry in by hand, being careful not to over-stir. Pour the batter into a well-greased muffin pan. Bake for 1 hour and 15 minutes.

4. When the top has browned and a muffin feels slightly firm, remove them from the oven. Let them sit in the pan for 10–15 minutes. An inserted toothpick should come out clean. Turn onto a rack to cool further.

8 FRESH FIGS

¼ CUP DRY SHERRY

1⅔ CUPS FLOUR

½ CUP ALMOND SLIVERS

1 TEASPOON SALT

1 TEASPOON BAKING SODA

1 TEASPOON CINNAMON

1 TEASPOON NUTMEG

1½ CUPS SUGAR

½ CUP VEGETABLE OIL

2 EGGS

Pork Sausage Scotch Eggs

YIELDS 4 SERVINGS

1. Combine the sausage, Worcestershire sauce, mustard, thyme, onion, cinnamon, and nutmeg in a bowl until well blended. Divide the mixture into six even portions.

2. Place a fryer over medium heat. Add the oil. While the oil comes to temperature, flatten the sausage into a patty. Use your fingers to stretch the sausage so it covers the egg. Roll each sausage-covered egg in bread crumbs and set it aside. Repeat with the remaining eggs.

3. Place two eggs in the oil. Cook for 6–8 minutes until the sausage is cooked and the bread crumbs are browned. Place the eggs on a rack over paper towels to drain. Repeat with the remaining eggs and serve hot or cold. Note: It's important to get a thin coat of sausage on the egg. If the layer is too thick, the sausage won't cook through before it browns. If this happens, preheat an oven to 350°F and bake the eggs for 10 minutes, or until they're done.

1 POUND LOOSE PORK SAUSAGE

1 TEASPOON WORCESTERSHIRE SAUCE

½ TEASPOON GROUND MUSTARD

1 TABLESPOON FRESH THYME

2 TABLESPOONS GRATED ONION

¼ TEASPOON GROUND CINNAMON

PINCH GROUND NUTMEG

1 CUP VEGETABLE OIL

4 HARD-BOILED EGGS, SHELLED

¾ CUP FINE, DRY BREAD CRUMBS

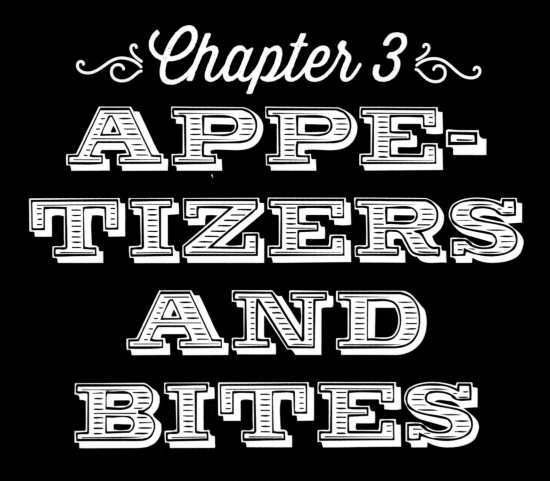

Chapter 3

APPE-TIZERS AND BITES

Blini

1. Whisk together the eggs, sugar, and salt in a large bowl. Sift the flour and baking powder over the bowl and pour the milk on top. Mix until blended.

2. Place a skillet over medium heat and brush the surface of the pan with a little of the oil.

3. Pour 2 tablespoons of batter onto the skillet surface and gently rotate the skillet on a slight angle to spread it out evenly.

4. When the edges start to crisp and the center looks dry, use a spatula to flip the pancake. Cook 1 minute, or until the other side is lightly browned, and then move it to a plate.

2 EGGS, BEATEN

1 TABLESPOON SUGAR

¼ TEASPOON SALT

½ CUP ALL-PURPOSE FLOUR

½ TEASPOON BAKING POWDER

2½ CUPS MILK

2 TABLESPOONS VEGETABLE OIL

¼ CUP SOFT BUTTER FOR SPREADING

Fried Tomato and Corn Salad

YIELDS 4–6 SERVINGS

1. Place the tomatoes in the freezer for at least 2 hours or overnight.

2. Use long tongs to hold the pepper over a burner set on high heat. Rotate and move the pepper until all of the skin has blackened and bubbled. Wrap it in a paper towel and roll it tightly in foil for 2 minutes. Remove the foil and use the paper towel to rub the skin off the pepper. Be careful not to burn yourself. Remove the stem and the seeds from the pepper and dice it finely.

3. Place a skillet over high heat and add the oil. Once it starts to smoke, add the tomatoes to the skillet. Wear an oven mitt around your wrist or use a splatter screen to protect yourself if the tomatoes pop. Shake the skillet back and forth frequently. Once the tomatoes start to thaw and release their juice, drain them and add the corn. Toss to combine and cook for 2–3 minutes. Drain again if necessary, add the onion and diced pepper, and cook for an additional 2–3 minutes. The onions should be soft.

4. Stir in the vinegar and season with salt, pepper, and the fresh cilantro and serve either hot, warm, or cold.

1 PINT CHERRY OR GRAPE TOMATOES

1 POBLANO PEPPER

1 TABLESPOON OLIVE OIL

KERNELS FROM 2 EARS OF SWEET CORN OR 2 CUPS FROZEN CORN

1 SMALL ONION

2 TEASPOONS SHERRY OR RICE WINE VINEGAR

SALT TO TASTE

PEPPER TO TASTE

1/3 CUP CHOPPED CILANTRO

Bulgur Salad with Roasted Chickpeas and Lemon

YIELDS 4 SERVINGS

1. Bring the water to a boil in a saucepan and add the bulgur and a pinch of salt. Let it sit for 20 minutes until all of the water has been absorbed.

2. Preheat oven to 400°F.

3. Place a skillet over medium heat. Once it is heated, add the onion, oil, lemon juice, bay leaves, cumin, turmeric, paprika, and cayenne. Stir until the onions are coated with the spices. Cook the onions for 5–7 minutes until they're soft and the spices smell toasted. Stir the chickpeas into the onions and cook until they start to sizzle.

4. Place the skillet into the middle of the oven for 20 minutes and stir halfway through. Remove the skillet from the oven, discard the bay leaves, and season with salt and pepper as necessary. Pour over the bulgur and serve while hot.

1¼ CUPS WATER

1 CUP COARSE BULGUR

1 MEDIUM RED ONION, THINLY SLICED

2 TABLESPOONS OLIVE OIL

JUICE FROM 1 LEMON

2 BAY LEAVES

1 TEASPOON CUMIN SEEDS

½ TEASPOON GROUND TURMERIC

½ TEASPOON GROUND PAPRIKA

1 PINCH CAYENNE PEPPER

1 15-OUNCE CAN CHICKPEAS, RINSED AND DRAINED

SALT TO TASTE

PEPPER TO TASTE

Bacon-Wrapped Stuffed Jalapeños

YIELDS 14 PIECES

1. Trim the woody part of the stem from the jalapeños. Cut the peppers open lengthwise and scoop out the seeds and the white veins. Spread a teaspoon or two of cream cheese onto each jalapeño half.

2. Starting at the thick end, wrap the bacon slice around the pepper. Spear with a toothpick to hold it in place. If the slice of bacon is too long, trim off the extra instead of wrapping it further.

3. Preheat oven to 375°F. Place a grill pan in the middle of the oven. Add the peppers and cook for 12–15 minutes, or until the bottom of the bacon is crispy.

4. Turn on the broiler and cook for 4–6 minutes until the cheese is bubbling and the bacon is crispy. Remove to a plate and let them rest before serving.

7 JALAPEÑOS

4 OUNCES CREAM CHEESE

14 SLICES BACON (APPROXIMATELY 1 POUND)

Griddle-Fried Plantains

YIELDS 18–24 PIECES

1. Sift the flour, baking powder, and salt together. Add the cold water to the dry ingredients and stir until it is lump-free. It should coat a spoon when dipped in the batter. Add a tablespoon of flour or water if necessary to get this texture.

2. Cut the ends off the plantains. Cut through the peel lengthwise several times and use the tip of a butter knife to pry off the peel. Cut the plantains in half and again in half lengthwise, and then cut each half into thirds. Use a rolling pin to flatten each plantain.

3. Place a griddle over medium-high heat. Once it is heated, pour 3 tablespoons of oil on the griddle and swirl so the surface is coated evenly. If the oil smokes, lower the heat until it stops smoking.

4. Dip each pounded strip into the batter and let the excess drain off. Place half of the slices of plantain on the griddle so they aren't touching. Fry each plantain for 1–2 minutes per side. They will darken more after they are removed from the oil. Add the rest of the oil and repeat with the rest of the plantains.

5. Sprinkle them with powdered sugar and eat while hot.

1 CUP FLOUR

½ TEASPOON BAKING POWDER

¼ TEASPOON SALT

¾ CUP COLD WATER

1½ POUNDS PLANTAINS

6 TABLESPOONS PEANUT OIL FOR FRYING

POWDERED SUGAR FOR SPRINKLING

Crispy Buffalo Chicken Bites

1. Preheat oven to 375°F and place a large griddle pan on the middle rack. Rinse the chicken and pat dry. Cut the chicken into 1½" cubes.

2. Whisk the butter, Tabasco sauce, garlic powder, vinegar, and salt together in a wide, shallow bowl. Place the corn flakes into another wide, shallow bowl.

3. Dip a handful of chicken pieces into the liquid mixture. Shake off the excess and drop them into the corn flakes. Roll them until coated and set aside. Repeat with the rest of the chicken.

4. Once the oven and griddle are hot, place the chicken on the griddle, spreading them out evenly so they barely touch. Cook for 6 minutes on the first side. Flip them and cook for another 6 minutes.

5. Remove them from the oven and let them cool as you place them on a serving platter with celery sticks and blue cheese dressing.

1½ POUNDS BONELESS, SKINLESS CHICKEN BREAST

¼ CUP BUTTER, MELTED

¼ CUP TABASCO SAUCE

1 TABLESPOON GARLIC POWDER

1 TABLESPOON APPLE CIDER VINEGAR

1 TEASPOON SALT

4 CUPS CORN FLAKES, CRUSHED

BLUE CHEESE DRESSING TO TASTE

Panko-Crusted Fried Ravioli

YIELDS 8–10 SERVINGS

1. Whisk the egg in a small bowl. In a separate bowl, combine the panko, spices, and cheese.

2. Dip each ravioli in the egg with one hand. Dip the ravioli in the panko mixture with the other hand.

3. Place a Dutch oven over medium heat and fill it with vegetable oil. Drop the ravioli in the oil and cook for 2 minutes on each side till they're lightly golden.

4. Remove them from the skillet and drain on paper towels. Serve with a bowl of warmed marinara sauce for dipping.

1 LARGE EGG

½ CUP PANKO OR BREAD CRUMBS

1 TEASPOON DRIED OREGANO

1 TEASPOON GARLIC POWDER

¼ TEASPOON BLACK PEPPER

½ TEASPOON SALT

2 TABLESPOONS SHREDDED PARMESAN CHEESE

1 PACKAGE FROZEN RAVIOLI, THAWED

2 CUPS VEGETABLE OIL

1 CUP MARINARA SAUCE, WARMED

Shiitake Mushroom Egg Rolls

YIELDS 20–25 EGG ROLLS

1. *For Sweet-and-Sour Dipping Sauce:* Whisk together ketchup, apple cider or white wine vinegar, fruit jam or jelly, and honey. Heat in a microwave. Whisk in cornstarch. If it doesn't thicken right away, heat a bit longer. Taste and add more jam as needed. Refrigerate until ready for use.

2. *For Egg Rolls:* Place a large skillet over medium-high heat. Once it's heated, add 1 tablespoon oil, cabbage, and carrots. Stir to combine. Cover and cook for 5 minutes, stirring every minute. Add the mushrooms, soy sauce, honey, garlic, ginger, vinegar, and sesame oil. Stir continually until the liquid has evaporated. Place in a colander. Cool for 15 minutes.

3. Remove the egg roll wrappers from the package and cover with a towel to prevent them from drying out. Whisk the cornstarch and cold water together until there are no lumps.

4. Place 1 wrapper as a diamond in front of you. Place 1 heaping tablespoon of the mixture 2" from the point nearest you. Fold the point over the filling and make one complete roll away from you. Tightly fold the right edge toward the middle, being careful not to tear the wrapper, but leaving no air between the wrapper and the right edge of the filling. Repeat with the left edge. Roll away from you until the point is sticking out. Dip your fingertips in the cornstarch mixture and rub along the outer edges. Roll to seal and place on a platter with the seam-side down. Refrigerate wrapped egg rolls for at least 4 hours.

5. Place a Dutch oven over medium heat. Add 2" of oil. Place as many egg rolls as you can in the pan without crowding. Cook for 1½–2 minutes. They'll darken after they come out. Serve hot with the Sweet-and-Sour Dipping Sauce.

SWEET-AND-SOUR DIPPING SAUCE

2 TABLESPOONS KETCHUP

¼ CUP APPLE CIDER OR WHITE WINE VINEGAR

2 TABLESPOONS OF ANY FRUIT JAM OR JELLY PLUS MORE AS NEEDED

¼ CUP HONEY

1 TABLESPOON CORNSTARCH

EGG ROLLS

1 TABLESPOON PEANUT OR VEGETABLE OIL

½ CABBAGE HEAD, SHREDDED

5 CARROTS, SHREDDED

¼ POUND SHIITAKE MUSHROOMS, THINLY SLICED

3 TABLESPOONS SOY SAUCE

½ TEASPOON HONEY

3 GARLIC CLOVES, MINCED

1" PIECE FRESH GINGER, PEELED AND SHREDDED

1 TABLESPOON RICE WINE VINEGAR

1 TEASPOON SESAME OIL

1 PACKAGE EGG ROLL WRAPPERS

1 TABLESPOON CORNSTARCH

¼ CUP COLD WATER

PEANUT OIL, AS NEEDED

Korean Hot Wings

1. Combine the soy sauce, water, brown sugar, and white wine in a small bowl. Heat in the microwave until the sugar is dissolved. Add the lemon juice, chili paste, honey, and serrano slices and let rest at room temperature for 1 hour or in the refrigerator for 3 days.

2. Rinse the chicken wings and pat dry. Place in a bowl and sprinkle with salt, pepper, and cornstarch to coat. Let set for 5 minutes. Place a wire rack over a baking sheet. Place 2 cups oil in a chicken fryer over medium heat. The oil is hot when a sprinkle of cornstarch causes the oil to bubble instantly.

3. Use tongs to slip four pieces of chicken into the pan. Cook on the first side for 2 minutes and the second for 1 minute. Place the wings on the wire rack and repeat. Bring the oil back to temperature between batches. Drain the oil, filter, and cool.

4. Add 1 tablespoon oil to a skillet over medium-low heat. Add the garlic and ginger and cook for 30 seconds. Add the sauce and stir continually for 30 seconds. Add the chicken wings to the pan and stir for 3 minutes until heated through and evenly coated. Serve warm.

3 TABLESPOONS SOY SAUCE

1 TABLESPOON WATER

1 TEASPOON BROWN SUGAR

1 TABLESPOON WHITE WINE

JUICE FROM 1 LEMON

1 TABLESPOON CHILI PASTE

2 TABLESPOONS HONEY

2 SERRANO PEPPERS, THINLY SLICED

2 POUNDS CHICKEN WINGS, SPLIT AT JOINT, WITHOUT TIPS

1 TEASPOON SALT

½ TEASPOON GROUND PEPPER

2 TABLESPOONS CORNSTARCH

2 CUPS PLUS 1 TABLESPOON CANOLA, CORN, OR PEANUT OIL

2 GARLIC CLOVES, SLICED

1 THUMB-SIZED PIECE FRESH GINGER, PEELED AND MATCHSTICKED

Deep-Fried Shrimp and Oysters

YIELDS 6–8 SERVINGS

1. Place a fryer or Dutch oven over medium to medium-high heat and add the oil. Make sure the temperature is 375°F. Combine the flour, salt, and Old Bay in a wide, shallow bowl. Beat the eggs in another wide, shallow bowl. Add the bread crumbs to a third wide, shallow bowl. Preheat the oven to its lowest setting. Place a wire rack on a cookie sheet in the middle of the oven.

2. Pat the oysters and shrimp dry. Dredge them in the flour mixture with one hand. Dip them in the egg with the other hand. Dredge them in the bread crumbs with the first hand and set on a clean, dry plate.

3. Once you have a plateful breaded, slide them into the oil and cook for 2 minutes, or until they're a light, golden brown. Place on the wire rack and sprinkle lightly with salt or more Old Bay. Repeat for remaining oysters and shrimp. Serve warm with cocktail sauce.

2 QUARTS SAFFLOWER OR CANOLA OIL

1 CUP ALL-PURPOSE FLOUR

2 TEASPOONS SALT

1 TEASPOON OLD BAY SEASONING

3 EGGS, BEATEN

1½ CUPS FINE BREAD CRUMBS OR PANKO

12 OUNCES SHUCKED OYSTERS, DRAINED AND COOLED

1 POUND MEDIUM SHRIMP, PEELED AND DEVEINED

COCKTAIL SAUCE TO TASTE

Deep-Fried Calamari

1. Thaw the calamari. Slice off the tentacles. Slice the tubes into ½"-wide rings. Pat dry with paper towels. Combine the cornmeal, cornstarch, Old Bay Seasoning, and the salt in a plastic bag. Add the calamari to the bag and shake till coated evenly.

2. Preheat oven to 175°F. Place a wire rack over a baking sheet in the middle of the oven. Place the oil in a fryer over medium-high heat. Once the oil is heated, carefully add a handful of calamari pieces. Cook for 2–3 minutes, or until they're lightly golden brown.

3. Remove the cooked calamari with a fryer basket or wire skimmer and place on the wire rack to drain.

1 POUND FROZEN CALAMARI, CLEANED

¼ CUP FINE CORNMEAL

2 TABLESPOONS CORNSTARCH

2 TEASPOONS OLD BAY SEASONING

½ TEASPOON SALT

1 QUART CANOLA OR SAFFLOWER OIL

Cheddar and Jalapeño Corn Sticks

YIELDS 14 STICKS

1. Preheat oven to 425°F. Place the corn stick pans on the middle rack.

2. Combine the dry ingredients in a large bowl. Whisk the milk and egg together. Add the milk mixture, cheese, scallions, and the jalapeños to the dry mixture and stir gently until everything is combined.

3. Remove the pans from the oven and use a brush to apply the melted butter. Pour the batter into the pans, being careful not to get any batter on the outside of the pans.

4. Bake for 12–15 minutes or until golden brown. Remove the sticks from the pan and let them cool for 5 minutes.

1 CUP YELLOW CORNMEAL

1 TEASPOON SUGAR

½ TEASPOON BAKING SODA

½ TEASPOON SALT

1 CUP MILK

1 EGG

1 CUP SHREDDED CHEDDAR CHEESE

2 SCALLIONS, FINELY CHOPPED

2 JALAPEÑOS, SEEDED AND MINCED

2 TABLESPOONS MELTED BUTTER

Jalapeño and Bell Pepper Vegetable Loaf

YIELDS 4–6 SERVINGS

1. Preheat oven to 350°F. Grease a loaf pan. Beat the eggs with the jalapeño, salt, and pepper in a bowl and set aside.

2. Place a skillet over medium-high heat. Add the oil, onion, and bell pepper. Cook for 5–7 minutes, stirring frequently. Add to the egg mixture. Stir the cheese, zucchini, carrot, and corn into the egg mixture.

3. Mix the flour and baking powder together in a large bowl. Stir in the egg mixture until combined but not smooth. Pour the mixture into the loaf pan and bake in the center of the oven for 25–30 minutes. Cool for 5 minutes before slicing and serving.

4 EGGS

1 JALAPEÑO, SEEDED AND DICED

1½ TEASPOONS SALT

¼ TEASPOON PEPPER

2 TABLESPOONS VEGETABLE OIL OR BUTTER

1 MEDIUM ONION, CHOPPED

½ RED BELL PEPPER, CHOPPED

½ CUP CRUMBLED FRESH CHEESE OR PARMESAN CHEESE

1 ZUCCHINI, GRATED

1 LARGE CARROT, PEELED AND GRATED

1 CUP FROZEN CORN

⅓ CUP FLOUR

½ TEASPOON BAKING POWDER

MUFFIN PAN POPOVERS

Muffin Pan Popovers

1. Preheat oven to 400°F. Grease each cup of the muffin pan generously with butter or solid vegetable shortening. Place the pan in the oven and bring to temperature.

2. Combine remaining ingredients in a blender and blend for slightly less than 1 minute. Scrape down the sides several times. When the pan is heated through, remove it from the oven and fill the cups halfway with batter.

3. Bake for 35–40 minutes. Popovers should be puffed and golden. To prevent them from collapsing, do not open the oven for 35 minutes. If they seem wet after 40 minutes, pierce with a butter knife, turn off the heat, and return them to the oven for 5 minutes.

BUTTER, AS NEEDED

2 EGGS, ROOM TEMPERATURE

1 CUP MILK, ROOM TEMPERATURE

1 TABLESPOON VEGETABLE OIL

1 CUP FLOUR

½ TEASPOON SALT

Mediterranean Olive Bread

YIELDS 1 LOAF

1. Preheat oven to 350°F. Place a rack in the lower third of the oven. Grease a 6-cup loaf pan with butter.

2. In a medium bowl, whisk together the flours, baking powder, and salt. Coarsely grind the dried herbs. Stir it into the flour mixture. In a large bowl, whisk eggs, milk, and oil until the yolks are incorporated. Add the flour mixture and the olives to the liquid mixture. Fold together until the dry ingredients are barely moistened.

3. Scrape the thick batter into the pan and spread evenly with a spatula. Bake for 40–45 minutes or until a toothpick inserted comes out clean. Cool for 5 minutes before slicing. Serve warm or cold.

BUTTER, AS NEEDED

1½ CUPS ALL-PURPOSE WHITE FLOUR

¾ CUP WHOLE-WHEAT FLOUR

1½ TEASPOONS BAKING POWDER

½ TEASPOON SALT

¾ TEASPOON DRIED ROSEMARY OR THYME

2 LARGE EGGS

1 CUP MILK

¼ CUP OLIVE OIL

½ CUP OLIVES, PITTED AND COARSELY CHOPPED

Corn Sticks with Local Honey

YIELDS 2 TRAYS OF CORN STICKS

1. Preheat oven to 400°F. Use a basting brush to thoroughly apply vegetable oil to the corn stick pans. Place the pans in the middle of the oven.

2. In a medium bowl, combine the flour, sugar, baking powder, baking soda, salt, and cornmeal. In a large bowl, whisk the egg, sour cream, milk, and 2 tablespoons vegetable oil. Once it is thoroughly combined and the egg is completely incorporated, pour the dry ingredients into the wet ingredients. Stir until the dry ingredients are moistened but not smooth.

3. Remove one of the pans. Use a small cup or spoon to fill the pan about two-thirds with batter. Place the first tray in the oven and repeat with the second. The pans should sizzle when you add the mix.

4. Bake the sticks for about 25 minutes or until golden brown. Carefully remove from the pan immediately. Serve hot with local honey.

VEGETABLE OIL, AS NEEDED, PLUS 2 TABLESPOONS

1/3 CUP FLOUR, SIFTED

1 TEASPOON SUGAR

1 TEASPOON BAKING POWDER

1/2 TEASPOON BAKING SODA

1/2 TEASPOON SALT

1 1/3 CUPS YELLOW CORNMEAL

1 EGG, BEATEN

1 CUP SOUR CREAM

3/4 CUP MILK

HONEY TO TASTE

Golden Buttermilk Cornbread

1. Place a skillet in the middle of the oven and preheat to 425°F. In a bowl, combine the cornmeal, salt, sugar, baking powder, and baking soda. Whisk together until well combined.

2. In a large bowl, whisk together the buttermilk and eggs. Once the yolks are completely incorporated, pour the dry ingredients into the wet ingredients. Stir gently to combine. Add more buttermilk if necessary to get a pourable consistency.

3. Add the vegetable oil to the skillet and swirl to coat the bottom and sides. Pour the batter into the skillet. You should hear the batter sizzle.

4. Bake for 20 minutes. If you press gently in the middle of the cornbread, it should spring back. Let it cool in the skillet for 10 minutes before serving.

2 CUPS YELLOW CORNMEAL

1 TEASPOON KOSHER SALT

¼ CUP SUGAR

2 TEASPOONS BAKING POWDER

½ TEASPOON BAKING SODA

1½ CUPS BUTTERMILK

2 EGGS

2 TABLESPOONS VEGETABLE OIL

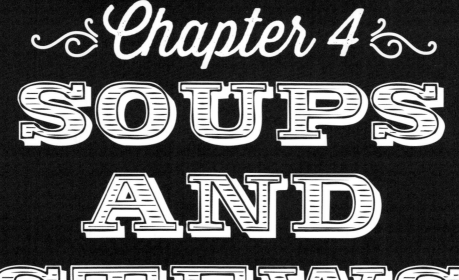

Chapter 4

SOUPS AND STEWS

Fresh-Roasted Tomato Soup

YIELDS 3–4 SERVINGS

1. Preheat oven to 325°F. Place the tomato halves in a large skillet. Add the garlic cloves and drizzle half the oil on top. Season liberally with salt and pepper. Place the pan in the oven and bake for 30 minutes.

2. Place a Dutch oven over medium-high heat. Add the rest of the oil, onions, and leeks. Cook for 10 minutes. Stir the tomatoes, garlic, and juices into the pan. Stir in the stock, vinegar, and herbs. Use a spoon to crush the tomatoes while they cook. Cook for 20 minutes. Use a stick blender to purée the tomato mixture, or let the soup cool slightly before adding to a stand mixer.

3. Boil again and let any unwanted liquid boil off. Turn off heat and stir in cream. Cover for 5 minutes and top with basil sprig, if desired, before serving.

10 PLUM TOMATOES, HALVED AND SEEDED

6 GARLIC CLOVES, SMASHED

¼ CUP OLIVE OIL

PINCH SALT

PINCH PEPPER

1 MEDIUM ONION, DICED

1 LARGE LEEK, CLEANED AND THINLY SLICED

3 CUPS VEGETABLE STOCK

1 TABLESPOON BALSAMIC VINEGAR

1 TABLESPOON FRESH BASIL OR THYME (OR 1 TEASPOON DRIED) PLUS 1 FRESH BASIL SPRIG FOR GARNISH IF DESIRED

1 CUP HEAVY CREAM

FRESH-ROASTED TOMATO SOUP

Onion and Garlic Soup

YIELDS 4 SERVINGS

1. Preheat oven to 350°F. Place a Dutch oven over medium heat. Once it's warmed, add the olive oil and onions. Stir frequently. If the onions start to stick, add more oil, and if they start to brown, reduce the heat.

2. Add the garlic to the pot. Stir to combine and cook for 3 minutes. Once you start to smell a warm garlic aroma, and before the garlic browns, turn off the heat.

3. Add the water and dried spices to the pot. Stir to combine. Cover and place in the middle of the oven. Cook for 2 hours.

4. Remove the bay leaf and cloves from the pot and either use a stick blender or carefully pour the soup into a heat-safe blender and purée. Taste and season accordingly. Toast the bread and then add one slice to each dish. Ladle soup over the bread to serve.

2 TABLESPOONS OLIVE OIL

3 SMALL YELLOW ONIONS, PEELED AND THINLY SLICED

2 LARGE HEADS GARLIC, PEELED AND SMASHED

2 QUARTS WATER

2 TEASPOONS SALT

LARGE PINCH PEPPER

2 WHOLE CLOVES

1 BAY LEAF

1 TEASPOON GROUND SAGE

1 TEASPOON DRIED THYME

1 TEASPOON GROUND MARJORAM

4 SLICES STALE BREAD

Spicy White Bean Chili

YIELDS 4–6 SERVINGS

1. Sort the beans and remove any debris. Place them in a large bowl and cover them with water by several inches and soak overnight. Drain and rinse the beans.

2. Place a Dutch oven over medium-high heat. Once it's heated through, add the oil and the onion. Cook the onions for 8–10 minutes.

3. Lower the heat to medium and stir in the garlic and the cumin. Cook for 1 minute before adding the turkey meat and the stock.

4. Bring to a simmer before adding the beans, cayenne powder, and chili powder. Reduce the heat to low and simmer for 4–5 hours, or until the beans are tender.

1 POUND CANNELLINI OR GREAT NORTHERN BEANS

WATER, AS NEEDED

1 TABLESPOON OLIVE OIL

1 MEDIUM ONION, FINELY CHOPPED

2 GARLIC CLOVES, MINCED

1 TEASPOON GROUND CUMIN

1 SMOKED TURKEY LEG, MEAT REMOVED AND CHOPPED

6 CUPS VEGETABLE STOCK

1 TEASPOON CAYENNE POWDER

½ TEASPOON CHILI POWDER

SWISS CHARD AND LENTIL SOUP

Swiss Chard and Lentil Soup

YIELDS 4 SERVINGS

1. Place a Dutch oven over medium heat. Add the broth and 2 cans of water. Sort the lentils and remove any debris. Once the liquid boils, add the lentils, cover, and boil again. Reduce the heat to low and cook for 20 minutes. Bite into a lentil; if the outside is soft, but the inside is still dense or crunchy, they're ready.

2. Rinse the chard well to remove any sand or dirt. Cut the stem out of the leaf and discard. Tear the leaves into 3" pieces. Once the lentils seem almost done, add the chard, mushroom, ginger, garlic powder, and coriander. Cover, return to a simmer, and cook for 5–10 minutes more, or until the lentils are no longer crunchy in the center. Add salt and pepper to taste.

2 14-OUNCE CANS VEGETABLE OR CHICKEN BROTH

WATER, AS NEEDED

1 CUP LENTILS

4 CUPS PACKED SWISS CHARD LEAVES

2 SHIITAKE MUSHROOMS, CHOPPED IN TINY PIECES

¼ TEASPOON GROUND GINGER

1 TEASPOON GARLIC POWDER

2 TEASPOONS DRIED CORIANDER

SALT TO TASTE

PEPPER TO TASTE

Hearty Homemade Mushroom Soup

YIELDS 4–6 SERVINGS

1. Place a Dutch oven over medium heat. Add 1 tablespoon of oil, 1 tablespoon of butter, and the onion. Cook for 5 minutes until it is softened but not yet starting to brown. Add garlic and cook for 1 minute, stirring continually. Stir in the stock.

2. Place a skillet over medium heat. Once it is heated, add 1 tablespoon of oil, 1 tablespoon of butter, and a handful of the sliced mushrooms. Sprinkle lightly with salt and pepper. Cook until they've reduced in size and are slightly browned. Remove from the skillet, transfer to the Dutch oven, and repeat with another batch of mushrooms.

3. Add the water to the skillet and scrape the bottom of the pan. Pour the water into the Dutch oven. Add the miso paste and stir well until combined. Once the Dutch oven starts to simmer, reduce the heat to low and simmer uncovered for 15 minutes. Add the sesame oil. Taste and add soy sauce or salt and pepper to taste.

5 TABLESPOONS OLIVE OIL

5 TABLESPOONS BUTTER

1 LARGE RED ONION, CHOPPED

2 GARLIC CLOVES, MINCED

1 QUART VEGGIE OR CHICKEN STOCK

1½ POUNDS MUSHROOMS, CLEANED AND SLICED

PINCH SALT

PINCH PEPPER

1 QUART WATER

2 TABLESPOONS MISO PASTE

1 TABLESPOON TOASTED SESAME OIL

SOY SAUCE TO TASTE

Sweet Potato and Peanut Soup

YIELDS 4–6 SERVINGS

1. Place a large pot over medium heat. Once it is warmed, add the oil and the onions. Cook for 5–7 minutes. Add the garlic and cook for 1 minute. Add the carrots, sweet potatoes, spices, and hot sauce and stir thoroughly. Cook for 5 minutes and add a little broth if necessary to keep the vegetables from sticking.

2. Increase the heat to medium-high and add the can of tomatoes and the broth. Stir the bottom of the pan. Bring to a boil. Reduce the heat to low and let the vegetables simmer for 25–30 minutes. Use a stick blender or potato masher to break up the potato chunks and make smooth.

3. Increase the heat to medium and stir in the peanut butter. Cook for 5 minutes until the peanut butter is thoroughly combined and warmed. Serve over rice with a sprinkle of scallion for garnish.

1 TABLESPOON OLIVE OIL

1 LARGE WHITE ONION, CHOPPED

6 CLOVES GARLIC, MINCED

3 CARROTS, CHOPPED

2 LARGE SWEET POTATOES, PEELED AND CUBED

1 TEASPOON SALT

1 TEASPOON CUMIN

1 TEASPOON THYME

1 TEASPOON SMOKED PAPRIKA

½ TEASPOON TURMERIC

¼ TEASPOON CINNAMON

GROUND BLACK PEPPER TO TASTE

½–1 TEASPOON HOT SAUCE

1 15-OUNCE CAN DICED TOMATOES

6 CUPS VEGETABLE OR CHICKEN BROTH

½ CUP PEANUT BUTTER

1 DICED SCALLION

Sardinian Minestrone Stew

YIELDS 4–6 SERVINGS

1. Place a Dutch oven over medium-high heat. Once the pan is heated, add 2 tablespoons olive oil and chopped vegetables. Cook for 10 minutes. Add 1 cup of stock and scrape the bottom of the pan.

2. Add the rest of the stock, the chickpeas, the tomato, and the greens and stir to combine.

3. Reduce the heat to low and cover. Cook for 1 hour. Add the pasta and cook for 10 minutes. Taste and add salt and pepper as needed. Once the pasta is al dente, serve it in large bowls with a drizzle of olive oil floating on top.

2 TABLESPOONS OLIVE OIL PLUS MORE AS NEEDED

1 CELERY STALK, CHOPPED

1 CARROT, CHOPPED

1 MEDIUM WHITE ONION, CHOPPED

2 QUARTS VEGETABLE OR CHICKEN STOCK

2 16-OUNCE CANS CHICKPEAS, RINSED AND DRAINED

1 15-OUNCE CAN CHOPPED TOMATOES

½ POUND ARUGULA, WASHED AND CHOPPED ROUGHLY

1 HEAD OF ENDIVE, SLICED IN LONG, THIN STRIPS

8 OUNCES SMALL PASTA

SALT TO TASTE

PEPPER TO TASTE

Crawfish Maque Choux

1. Place the crawfish or peeled shrimp in a large glass bowl. Add the wine, lemon juice, and salt and toss to combine. Let it marinate for 20 minutes. Stand each ear of corn on end and cut the kernels off. Then run the back of the knife down the cobs to get the corn milk and corn germ out of the cob.

2. Place a large skillet over medium heat. Add the bacon drippings and bell pepper and cook for 2 minutes, stirring frequently. Add the chopped onion and cook until it is translucent and just starting to brown. Remove the vegetables to another bowl.

3. Add the corn, butter, cream, and stock to the skillet. Stir continuously for 10 minutes until some of the stock has evaporated. Add the tomatoes and cook for 5 minutes.

4. Discard the marinade from the shellfish and add the meat to the skillet. Cook while stirring frequently for 5 minutes. If the mixture seems a bit dry, add some more stock or water. Add the black pepper and the reserved vegetables. Taste before adding Tabasco sauce and salt if necessary. Garnish with parsley. Serve in bowls immediately.

2 12-OUNCE PACKAGES FROZEN CRAWFISH TAILS OR 2 POUNDS MEDIUM SHRIMP

½ CUP DRY WHITE WINE

JUICE FROM 1 LEMON

½ TEASPOON SALT

8 EARS WHITE CORN ON THE COB

3 TABLESPOONS BACON DRIPPINGS OR OLIVE OIL

1 GREEN BELL PEPPER, FINELY CHOPPED

1 LARGE WHITE ONION, FINELY CHOPPED

¼ CUP BUTTER

2 TABLESPOONS HEAVY CREAM OR WHOLE MILK

2 CUPS CHICKEN STOCK

1 15-OUNCE CAN DICED TOMATOES, DRAINED

1 TEASPOON GROUND BLACK PEPPER

½ TEASPOON TABASCO SAUCE

2 TABLESPOONS CHOPPED PARSLEY

Smoked Turkey Chili

1. Sort beans and remove any debris. Place the beans in a large pot and cover with cold water by 3". Cover the pan and place it over high heat and bring to a boil. Boil for 10 minutes and remove from the heat. Cover and let soak for at least 8 hours. Drain, rinse the beans, and set aside.

2. Put the pepper strips in a bowl and cover with hot water. Soak for 30 minutes. Transfer the peppers to a blender and add 1 cup of the soaking water. Purée to get a fine texture. Discard the rest of the water.

3. Preheat oven to 325°F. Place a Dutch oven over medium heat and add the onion and oil. Cook for 7–10 minutes, stirring frequently. Add the garlic and cumin. Stir continually for 1 minute, add the pepper purée, and stir to combine.

4. Cut the meat off the turkey leg and chop into small pieces. Stir it into the pot. Add the soaked beans and 4 cups vegetable stock. Cover and bring the beans to a boil. Turn off the heat and place in the oven.

5. Cook for 3–4 hours. If the beans start to dry out, add more broth. Stir the beans every 45 minutes. If the beans seem soupy, remove the lid after 2 hours of cooking to let the liquid evaporate.

1 POUND CANNELLINI OR GREAT NORTHERN BEANS

WATER, AS NEEDED

6 DRIED NEW MEXICO CHILIES, STEMMED, SEEDED, CUT IN STRIPS

1 MEDIUM YELLOW ONION, CHOPPED

1 TABLESPOON OLIVE OIL

2 GARLIC CLOVES, MINCED

2 TEASPOONS GROUND CUMIN

1 SMOKED TURKEY LEG

4-6 CUPS VEGETABLE STOCK

SALT TO TASTE

PEPPER TO TASTE

SMOKED TURKEY CHILI

Dutch Oven Gumbo

1. Preheat oven to 350°F. Mix all the spices together and rub over the pieces of chicken. Place in a Dutch oven. Cut the sausage at an angle into ¼"-thick slices. Sprinkle the sausage over the chicken. Cook in the oven for 40 minutes. Pour off all the fat.

2. Save the sausage on a platter. Lay the chicken pieces out to cool. Once it is cool to the touch, remove all the meat from the bones and set the bones and skin aside for making stock.

3. Place the chicken meat and sausage back in the Dutch oven. Add the bay leaves and any leftover seasoning mix to the pan. Tuck the garlic cloves around the meat with the bay leaves. Cover with chicken stock by 2". Turn the heat to medium-high, cover, and boil. Lower the heat to a simmer and cook for 45 minutes. Stir to prevent sticking.

4. Add the okra and cook for 30 minutes. Sprinkle the shrimp on top; cut up the crabmeat and add to the pan. Cook for 6–8 minutes. Taste and add salt if necessary. Ladle the gumbo over rice in a bowl. Garnish with parsley. Serve with Tabasco and crusty bread.

2 TEASPOONS PAPRIKA

1 TEASPOON GARLIC POWDER

½ TEASPOON DRIED OREGANO

½ TEASPOON BLACK PEPPER

½ TEASPOON DRIED THYME

½ TEASPOON ONION POWDER

¼ TEASPOON CAYENNE POWDER

1 TEASPOON SALT

1 SMALL FRYING CHICKEN, CUT INTO 10 PIECES

1 POUND ANDOUILLE SAUSAGE

2 BAY LEAVES

3 GARLIC CLOVES, CHOPPED

2 QUARTS CHICKEN STOCK

½ POUND OKRA, CUT INTO ½" ROUNDS

1 POUND SHELLED SHRIMP

8 OUNCES CRABMEAT

½ CUP COOKED LONG-GRAIN RICE PER PERSON

½ CUP FRESH PARSLEY, CHOPPED

Indonesian Chicken Soup

YIELDS 6–8 SERVINGS

1. Place a large Dutch oven over medium-high heat. Rinse the chicken and place breast-side down in the pan. Add the water. Cut off the base and the tips of the lemongrass and cut the stalk into 4" pieces. Tuck around the chicken. Sprinkle the zest in the water. Bring to a boil and skim the foam off the surface.

2. Once it boils, reduce the heat to low and cover the pan with a lid. Cook for 45 minutes and skim the foam off the top. Meanwhile, combine all of the remaining ingredients except noodles, lime, and cilantro in a food processor. Pulse for several minutes to create a creamy paste.

3. Once the chicken is cooked so the legs are loose, remove the chicken to a platter or bowl. Increase the heat to medium and stir in the flavoring paste.

4. Remove the skin from the chicken and discard. Cut off the chicken in large chunks and discard the bones. Return the chicken to the pot and cook for 10 minutes. Cook the glass noodles according to package directions and serve in bowls topped with the soup, with lime juice and cilantro as garnish.

1 3–3½-POUND CHICKEN

2 QUARTS WATER

2 STALKS LEMONGRASS

ZEST FROM 1 LIME

1 TEASPOON SALT

2 JALAPEÑO PEPPERS OR 1 SERRANO PEPPER

1 TEASPOON GROUND CORIANDER

1 TEASPOON GROUND CUMIN

3 SHALLOTS, PEELED

3 GARLIC CLOVES

1 TEASPOON GROUND TURMERIC

2" PIECE GINGER, PEELED

1 PACKAGE GLASS NOODLES

JUICE FROM 1 LIME

¼ CUP CHOPPED CILANTRO

Solyanka

YIELDS 4–6 SERVINGS

1. Place the cucumbers in a colander or strainer. Sprinkle salt over the cucumbers and toss till coated. Let them sit in the colander for at least 20 minutes.

2. Preheat oven to 350°F. Place a Dutch oven over medium heat. Add the oil and beef. Cook for 6 minutes. Turn so all the beef is browned.

3. Remove the beef from the pan and add the bacon. Cook until it is brown but not crispy. Add the sausages and onion and cook for 10–12 minutes.

4. Once the sausages are browned, return the reserved meat and add 6 cups of water. Bring it to a boil and reduce the heat to low. Simmer for 10 minutes.

5. Stir in the cucumbers, tomato paste, olives, bay leaves, and capers. Place in the middle of the oven and cook for 30 minutes. Remove when the sausages are cooked through. Stir in the sour cream. Ladle into bowls and serve while warm with lemon slices and chopped dill as garnish.

1 POUND CUCUMBERS, DICED

2 TABLESPOONS SALT

2 TABLESPOONS VEGETABLE OIL

12 OUNCES STEW MEAT CHUNKS, DICED

8 OUNCES BACON, SLICED INTO 1" PIECES

4 SMOKED PORK SAUSAGES

1 LARGE ONION, QUARTERED AND SLICED

6 CUPS WATER

2 TABLESPOONS TOMATO PASTE

1 CUP BLACK OLIVES

3 BAY LEAVES

¼ CUP CAPERS

1 CUP SOUR CREAM

1 LEMON, THINLY SLICED

1 BUNCH FRESH DILL, CHOPPED

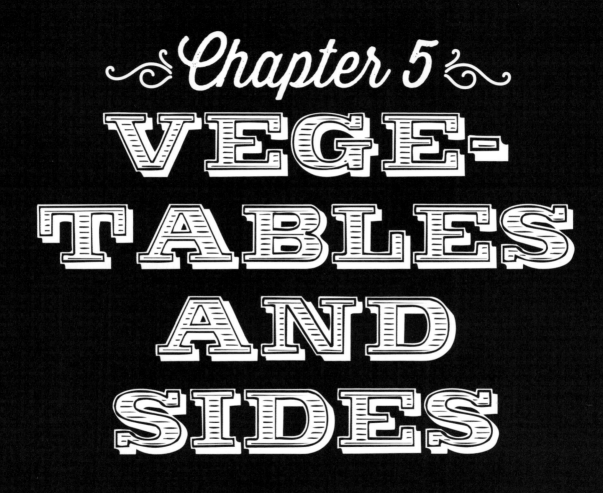

Chapter 5
VEGE-TABLES AND SIDES

Oven-Fried Potatoes

1. Preheat oven to 400°F. Place a skillet in the middle of the oven.

2. Scrub the potatoes clean and pat dry with a lint-free towel. Cut each potato into ¼" or ⅜" slices. Cut the slices into strips the same width. Cut those strips into cubes. Place into a bowl and drizzle with olive oil. Sprinkle with salt and pepper and toss so they're evenly coated.

3. Pour potatoes into the warm skillet so there is one even layer on the bottom. Place the skillet in the middle of the oven and bake for 30 minutes. Stir once or twice. The potatoes should be soft in the middle with crispy edges. Serve while hot.

2 MEDIUM YUKON GOLD POTATOES

1 TABLESPOON OLIVE OIL

SALT TO TASTE

PEPPER TO TASTE

Stir-Fried Asparagus

YIELDS 4 SERVINGS

1. Wash the asparagus and snap off the bottoms. Cut them into 1" slices on an angle.

2. Place a skillet over medium heat. Once it has heated, add the oil and the asparagus. Sprinkle them with salt and pepper and stir continually for 2 minutes until they're coated.

3. Add 2 tablespoons of water or chicken broth and cover. Cook for 2 minutes.

4. Turn off the heat but keep the skillet covered for 3 minutes or until tender. Serve while hot.

1 POUND THIN ASPARAGUS

2 TABLESPOONS OLIVE OIL

PINCH SALT

PINCH PEPPER

2 TABLESPOONS WATER OR CHICKEN BROTH

STIR-FRIED ASPARAGUS

Sautéed Mushrooms

YIELDS 4 SERVINGS

1. Place a large skillet over medium heat. Add 1 tablespoon of butter and 1 tablespoon of oil.

2. Once the butter has stopped foaming, add one large handful of mushrooms. Sprinkle them lightly with salt and pepper. Cook for several minutes on each side, or until they've shrunk in size and turned dark brown. Remove from skillet and keep them warm.

3. Repeat with the rest of the butter, oil, and mushrooms until all of the mushrooms are cooked.

4. If the skillet is dry, add a small amount of oil. Add the shallots and stir frequently for 5 minutes, or until they're soft and starting to brown.

5. Return the mushrooms to the skillet and stir occasionally for 3 minutes, or until the mushrooms are hot again. Serve hot.

3 TABLESPOONS BUTTER

3 TABLESPOONS OLIVE OIL

1 POUND MUSHROOMS, SLICED

PINCH SALT

PINCH PEPPER

4 LARGE SHALLOTS, MINCED

Sautéed Okra and Tomatoes

YIELDS 6–8 SERVINGS

1. Wash the okra pods, cut off the stem ends, and slice the pods into ¼" slices. Pat them dry to prevent oil splatters. Place a skillet over medium-high heat. Once it is heated, add the oil, onion, and okra. Cook them for several minutes on each side. The onion should be golden brown about the same time that the okra is crispy on the cut sides.

2. Add the tomatoes and garlic, stirring continually for 2–3 minutes, or just until the tomatoes are cooked through. Pour into a bowl and sprinkle with the apple cider vinegar. Stir to combine and taste before adding salt and pepper.

1 POUND OKRA PODS, STEMMED AND SLICED INTO RINGS

3 TABLESPOONS VEGETABLE OIL

1 SMALL YELLOW ONION, CHOPPED

3 LARGE FRESH TOMATOES, SEEDED AND CHOPPED

2 GARLIC CLOVES, MINCED

1 TABLESPOON APPLE CIDER VINEGAR

SALT TO TASTE

PEPPER TO TASTE

Sautéed Radishes with Scallions

YIELDS 4 SERVINGS

1. Place a skillet over medium heat. When it is heated, add the butter. Once the butter has melted, add the radishes and stir frequently for 2–3 minutes, or until the radishes have started to soften.

2. Sprinkle the scallion over the radishes and pour the chicken broth into the skillet. Cover the skillet and let the radishes cook for about 4 minutes.

3. Once the radishes are tender, uncover and increase the heat. Boil rapidly until the liquid has evaporated. Stir frequently to keep them from sticking. Sprinkle lightly with salt and serve immediately.

1 TABLESPOON BUTTER

2 BUNCHES RED RADISHES, CLEANED, STEMMED, QUARTERED

1 SCALLION, CHOPPED INTO RINGS

½ CUP CHICKEN STOCK

SALT TO TASTE

CARAMELIZED CARROTS

Caramelized Carrots

1. Place a skillet over medium heat. Add the carrots and apple juice. Add enough water to just cover the carrots. Simmer for about 5–7 minutes, or until the thickest pieces can be pierced with a fork. Drain off the water.

2. Use a Microplane or zester to remove about 1 tablespoon of peel from the lemon. Squeeze the lemon to get 2 tablespoons of juice. Place the skillet back over medium heat and add the lemon zest, lemon juice, butter, oil, and brown sugar. Stir to combine. Once it starts to bubble, reduce the heat slightly and stir frequently to keep the carrots from sticking. Cook for about 5 minutes. They should be soft and glazed. Serve while hot and garnish with the almonds.

1 POUND CARROTS, PEELED AND CUT INTO ¼"-THICK SLICES

½ CUP APPLE JUICE

WATER, AS NEEDED

1 LEMON

2 TABLESPOONS BUTTER

2 TABLESPOONS OLIVE OIL

¼ CUP BROWN SUGAR

¼ CUP SLIVERED OR SLICED ALMONDS

Roasted Broccoli with Parmesan

YIELDS 6 SERVINGS

1. Preheat oven to 450°F. Place a skillet in the middle of the oven. Trim the bottoms off the broccoli stems. Peel the stems and cut them into skinny florets. Place in a bowl and toss with the oil, pepper flakes, salt, and pepper. Spread the broccoli throughout the skillet. Sprinkle the cheese over the broccoli.

2. Place the pan in the middle of the oven and cook for 20–25 minutes, or until the stems have softened.

3. Place the broccoli on a serving platter. Pour the vinegar into the skillet and stir, scraping the caramelized bits off the bottom. Pour the pan juices over the broccoli and serve.

3 POUNDS BROCCOLI

6 TABLESPOONS OLIVE OIL

¾ TEASPOON RED PEPPER FLAKES

PINCH SALT

PINCH PEPPER

¾ CUP GRATED PARMESAN CHEESE

⅓ CUP WHITE WINE VINEGAR

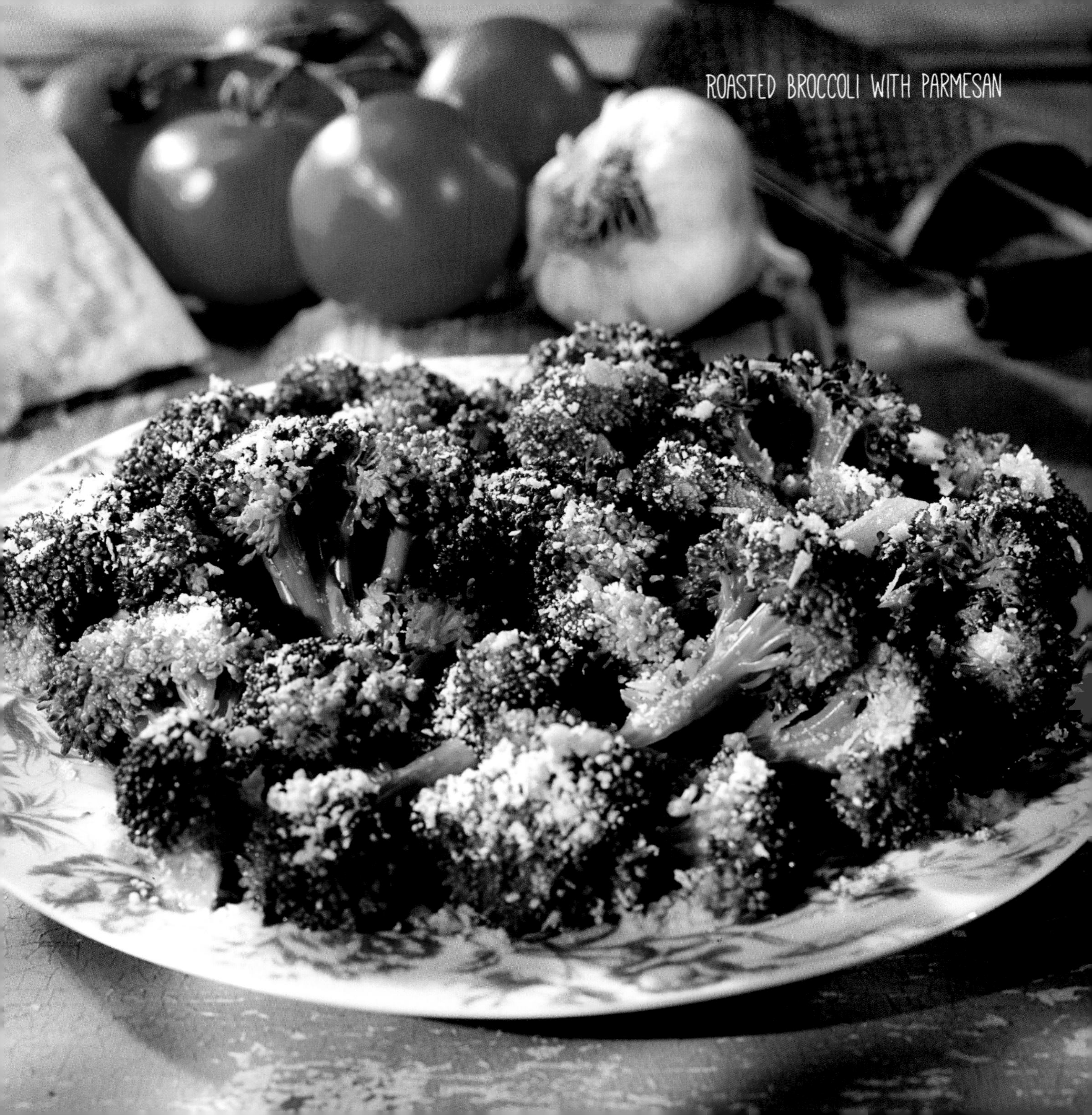
ROASTED BROCCOLI WITH PARMESAN

Cauliflower with Chickpeas and Mustard Seeds

YIELDS 6–8 SERVINGS

1. Place a skillet over medium heat. Once the skillet is heated add the onion, olive oil, and mustard seeds. Stir frequently and let the onion cook until it starts to turn brown.

2. Add the cauliflower florets to the skillet with a sprinkle of salt.

3. Stir to combine and cook for 4 minutes. Add the chickpeas to the skillet with the white wine. Stir to combine.

4. Cover the skillet and cook for 3–4 minutes. Remove the lid and let the liquid evaporate. Serve when the cauliflower is fork tender.

1 MEDIUM WHITE ONION, CHOPPED

1 TABLESPOON OLIVE OIL

5 TABLESPOONS YELLOW OR BLACK MUSTARD SEEDS

1 HEAD CAULIFLOWER, DIVIDED INTO FLORETS

PINCH SALT

1 CAN CHICKPEAS, DRAINED AND RINSED

¼ CUP WHITE WINE

Asian Potatoes with Chili and Shallots

1. Mince the shallots and chilies finely. Place in a bowl, sprinkle with ½ teaspoon salt, and toss to combine. Let sit for 10 minutes. Smash the vegetables into a slight paste.

2. Place a skillet over medium-high heat. Add the oil, then add the potatoes when the oil is warmed. Nudge them for 3 minutes to keep from sticking. Turn them over and cook for 3–5 minutes. Once the outsides are crispy, place on paper towels to drain.

3. Drain off most of the oil. Place over medium heat and add the paste. Stir continually for 4–5 minutes. Once it smells toasty, add the potatoes and toss until they're well coated and warmed. Sprinkle vinegar and pinch of salt over the potatoes and serve immediately.

3 SHALLOTS OR 1 SMALL YELLOW ONION

2 SERRANO CHILIES

½ TEASPOON PLUS 1 PINCH SALT

¼ CUP PEANUT OIL

1½ POUNDS YUKON GOLD POTATOES, CUT INTO 6 WEDGES

1 TEASPOON APPLE CIDER VINEGAR

Icelandic Sugar-Glazed Potatoes

YIELDS 8–10 SERVINGS

1. Place a large pan of water over high heat. Boil the potatoes whole for 20 minutes. When you can insert a knife to the middle of the potato, it is ready. Remove them to cool and reserve the cooking water. Peel the skins and cut the potatoes into thick slices.

2. Place a skillet over medium heat. Add the sugar and butter. If the sugar starts to smoke, lower the temperature. Whisk them together. Add 1–3 tablespoons of water that the potatoes were boiled in.

3. Place the potatoes in the skillet one at a time and stir to coat. If the mixture won't coat, increase the temperature slightly and add 1–2 tablespoons of water. When all of the potatoes are coated in sugar and warm, serve.

WATER, AS NEEDED

2 POUNDS WAXY POTATOES

4 TABLESPOONS SUGAR

3 TABLESPOONS BUTTER

¼ CUP VERY HOT WATER

Pommes Fondantes

YIELDS 4-6 SERVINGS

1. Wash the potatoes and remove the eyes. Arrange as many as possible in a 10" or 12" skillet. Add all of the remaining ingredients. Bring the pan to a boil, reduce the heat to medium, then cover with a lid that is slightly ajar. Cook the potatoes for 15–20 minutes or until a fork can be inserted easily.

2. Make sure the liquid covers half of the potatoes and add more broth if necessary. Use the bottom of a sturdy drinking glass to lightly smash the potatoes so the skins barely crack. Place the pan over medium-high heat and cook until all of the liquid has evaporated and the potatoes are brown on one side, about 10–12 minutes.

3. Use a pair of tongs to gently turn the potatoes. Cook for 5–7 minutes until brown on the other side. If necessary, add another tablespoon of olive oil.

4. Remove the pan from the heat and let the potatoes rest for about 5 minutes before sprinkling with a little extra salt to serve.

2 POUNDS BABY RED POTATOES

2 CUPS CHICKEN OR VEGETABLE BROTH

2 TABLESPOONS OLIVE OIL

1 TABLESPOON BUTTER

1 TABLESPOON CHOPPED SORREL OR THYME

½ TEASPOON SALT

Swiss Chard with Balsamic Vinegar

YIELDS 2–3 SERVINGS

1. Run the chard under cold water to remove any leftover dirt. Cut the thick part of the stem out of the leaves and set aside. Tear the leaves into several pieces and place on a towel. Chop the stems into ½" pieces.

2. Place a skillet over medium heat. Once it is hot, add the oil, the stem pieces, and the onion. Cook for 5–7 minutes, or until the onion is translucent and just starting to brown.

3. Add the garlic, pepper flakes, vinegar, nutmeg, and stock. Stir to combine and bring to a boil.

4. Add the leaves and stir, cooking for 2–3 minutes before covering. They should be starting to wilt. Cook for 4–5 minutes, or until the leaves are cooked through and limp.

5. Remove the lid and stir frequently as the liquid evaporates. Taste and add more vinegar, salt, or pepper as needed. Serve immediately.

1 POUND SWISS CHARD

1 TABLESPOON OLIVE OIL

½ SMALL ONION, CHOPPED

1 GARLIC CLOVE, MINCED

PINCH CRUSHED RED PEPPER FLAKES

1 TABLESPOON CIDER OR BALSAMIC VINEGAR

PINCH NUTMEG

½ CUP CHICKEN STOCK

SALT TO TASTE

PEPPER TO TASTE

Kale with Crispy Bacon and Roma Tomatoes

YIELDS 6–8 SERVINGS

1. Strip all the stems from the leaves and discard. Wash the leaves thoroughly and shake or drain until fairly dry. Chop or tear the leaves into large pieces and set aside.

2. Place a large skillet over medium-high heat. When heated, add the strips of bacon. Cook till crisp, remove from the pan, and let cool. Pour off all but 1 tablespoon of the bacon fat.

3. Add the olive oil and chopped onion to the skillet with the bacon fat. Cook for 5–7 minutes, or until the onion is soft and starting to brown. Stir in the minced garlic clove.

4. Add a large bunch of kale to the skillet and sprinkle with salt and pepper. Cover with a lid for 1 minute to wilt the kale. Use a spoon to move the wilted kale to the outsides of the skillet. Repeat until all of the kale has been added. Stir frequently and cook for 15–20 minutes till tender.

5. Crumble the cooked bacon and sprinkle on top with the tomato. Sprinkle the balsamic vinegar over the kale and toss to combine. Remove to a bowl and serve immediately.

2 POUNDS KALE

4 SLICES BACON

1 TABLESPOON OLIVE OIL

1 SMALL ONION, CHOPPED

2 GARLIC CLOVES, MINCED

SALT TO TASTE

PEPPER TO TASTE

2 ROMA TOMATOES, SEEDED AND CHOPPED

2 TABLESPOONS BALSAMIC VINEGAR

Spicy Mustard Greens

1. Remove the veins from the leaves and rinse them thoroughly in cold water. Shake dry and tear into large pieces.

2. Place a skillet over medium-high heat. Once it's heated, add the oil and onion. Stir frequently until they're soft and starting to turn brown, about 10 minutes.

3. Stir in the garlic, cumin, and crushed red pepper and cook for 3 minutes.

4. Add one batch of the greens and cover for 1–2 minutes until the greens wilt. Repeat with the other batches until all the greens have been added and have wilted.

5. Add the broth, cover, and reduce the heat to low. Let the greens cook for 30–45 minutes. They should be very tender. Taste before adding salt and pepper. Serve while hot with spicy vinegar for people to garnish as they wish.

2 LARGE BUNCHES MUSTARD GREENS

3 TABLESPOONS OLIVE OIL

2 MEDIUM ONIONS, CHOPPED

6 GARLIC CLOVES, MINCED

1 TEASPOON GROUND CUMIN

1 TEASPOON DRIED CRUSHED RED PEPPER FLAKES

1 CUP CHICKEN OR VEGETABLE BROTH

SALT AND PEPPER TO TASTE

SPICY VINEGAR AS CONDIMENT

Spinach with Greek Yogurt and Paneer

YIELDS 4 SERVINGS

1. Place a skillet over medium heat. Once it is warm, add the oil and the onion. Stir the onion frequently for 4–5 minutes or until translucent.

2. Add the dried spices and stir continually for 2 minutes. The spices should be very fragrant.

3. Add the spinach to the skillet and stir, scraping any bits of spice off the bottom if necessary. Add the jalapeño, garlic, tomato, and cilantro. Cook for 10 minutes.

4. Add the salt and broth to the skillet and stir to combine. Let the liquid evaporate before stirring in the yogurt and cheese. Stir for 1–2 minutes until the cheese and yogurt are warmed. Serve immediately over cooked basmati rice.

1 TABLESPOON VEGETABLE OIL

1 SMALL YELLOW ONION, CHOPPED

½ TEASPOON GROUND TURMERIC

1 TEASPOON GROUND CUMIN

1 TEASPOON GARAM MASALA POWDER

1 POUND FROZEN SPINACH, THAWED, SQUEEZED, AND CHOPPED

1 GREEN JALAPEÑO (OPTIONAL), SEEDED AND CHOPPED

1 GARLIC CLOVE, MINCED

1 SMALL TOMATO, CHOPPED

¼ CUP CHOPPED CILANTRO

1 TEASPOON SALT

12 OUNCES CHICKEN BROTH

1 CUP PLAIN GREEK YOGURT

8 OUNCES PANEER

Romanesco with Mushroom and Wine Sauce

YIELDS 4–6 SERVINGS

1. Rinse the Romanesco and break the clusters, or curds, off the stalks. Add salt to a pot of water with a steamer basket and bring to a boil over high heat. Once the water comes to a boil, add the Romanesco and cover. Cook for 5 minutes. Remove from the water and drain well.

2. Place a skillet over medium heat and add the mushrooms, shallots, and butter. Cook for 10–12 minutes, stirring every few minutes, until the shallots and mushrooms have softened and browned. Add the wine and mustard and reduce the heat to low.

3. After the Romanesco has drained, add it to the skillet. Cook uncovered for an additional 5–10 minutes until the Romanesco has reached the desired tenderness and the wine sauce has reduced.

1 HEAD ROMANESCO

1 TEASPOON SALT

WATER, AS NEEDED

1 POUND BUTTON MUSHROOMS, SLICED

3 SHALLOTS OR 1 SMALL YELLOW OR RED ONION, SLICED

3 TABLESPOONS BUTTER OR OLIVE OIL

½ CUP PORT OR OTHER HEAVY RED WINE

½ TEASPOON DIJON MUSTARD

Grilled Okra

1. Prepare a high-heat grill pan. Combine the salt, sugar, and spices in a small bowl.

2. Rinse the okra in cold water and trim off the stem, but don't cut into the pod. Shake dry and place into a large bowl. Drizzle the oil over the okra and toss with your hands to coat.

3. Sprinkle the spice mix over the okra, tossing so it's coated evenly. Insert skewers perpendicularly through the pods.

4. Place skewers on the grill and cook for 2–4 minutes on each side, using tongs to turn them over. Transfer to a platter and serve immediately.

1 TEASPOON KOSHER SALT (½ TEASPOON TABLE SALT)

1 TEASPOON WHITE SUGAR

2 TEASPOONS SWEET PAPRIKA

1 TEASPOON GROUND CORIANDER

½ TEASPOON GROUND BLACK PEPPER

½ TEASPOON CAYENNE PEPPER

¼ TEASPOON CELERY SEED

1 POUND OKRA

2 TABLESPOONS VEGETABLE OIL

Garlic Confit

YIELDS ½ CUP

1. Preheat oven to 350°F.

2. Peel all of the garlic cloves and place them in a small skillet. Pour the olive oil on top of the garlic cloves.

3. Bake the garlic for 45 minutes to 1 hour, or until the garlic is soft and golden brown.

1 HEAD GARLIC

½ CUP OLIVE OIL

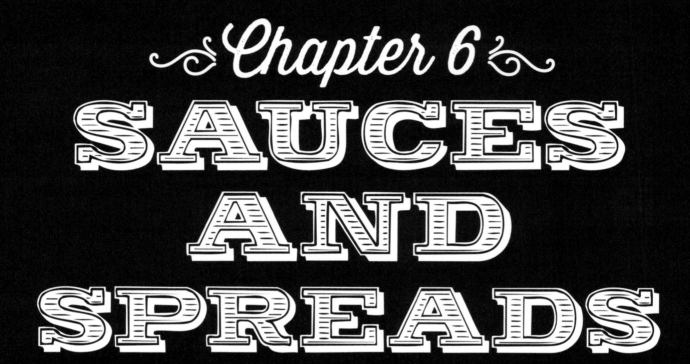

Chapter 6
SAUCES AND SPREADS

Cajun Roux

1. Place a skillet over medium heat. Once it is heated, add the oil. Stir the oil with a whisk in one hand while you slowly add the flour with the other. Once all of the flour is added, stir continuously for up to 25 minutes. Use the whisk to scrape the edges of the skillet to prevent the roux from browning.

2. Once the roux looks just darker than peanut butter, turn off the heat and add the vegetables. The sugars in the vegetables, and the residual heat from the hot skillet, will permit the roux to get darker and finish cooking.

1 CUP VEGETABLE OIL OR PEANUT OIL

1¼ CUPS ALL-PURPOSE FLOUR

1 ONION, CHOPPED

1 BELL PEPPER, CHOPPED

3 CELERY STALKS, CHOPPED

2 CARROTS, CHOPPED

Beurre Blanc

YIELDS 4 TABLESPOONS

1. Place a skillet over medium heat. Once it is heated, add the shallot and wine. Stir continually until the liquid has reduced by half and is starting to get a syrup-like consistency.

2. Reduce the heat to low and add 1 tablespoon of butter. Whisk the sauce continually until the butter is almost melted. Add the next pat while there are bits of butter in the skillet. Repeat until all of the butter is melted and the sauce can easily coat the back of a spoon.

3. Whisk in the lemon juice and taste before seasoning with salt and pepper. Serve immediately.

1 SHALLOT, MINCED

2 TABLESPOONS WHITE WINE

4 TABLESPOONS BUTTER, CUT INTO 1-TABLESPOON SECTIONS

JUICE FROM 1 LEMON

SALT TO TASTE

PEPPER TO TASTE

Chipotle Orange Sauce

YIELDS 1 CUP

1. Place a skillet over medium-high heat. Once it is heated, add the oil and the onion. Cook for 5–7 minutes, or until the onion has softened and has started to turn brown.

2. Stir in the remaining ingredients and simmer for 10 minutes, or until it has reduced and thickened. Taste and season with salt as necessary.

1 TEASPOON VEGETABLE OIL

½ SMALL ONION, FINELY CHOPPED

1 7-OUNCE CAN CHIPOTLE IN ADOBO SAUCE

1 CUP ORANGE JUICE

JUICE FROM 1 LIME

1 TEASPOON GROUND CUMIN

2 GARLIC CLOVES, MINCED

2 TABLESPOONS BROWN SUGAR

SALT TO TASTE

Toasted Peanut Sauce

YIELDS 3 CUPS

1. Place an enameled pot over medium heat. Add all the ingredients and bring to a boil, whisking continually.

2. Reduce the heat to low and simmer for 4 minutes, stirring occasionally.

3. Remove from the heat and serve immediately or place in an airtight container in the refrigerator for up to 1 month. (Refrigerated sauce will be thick, but will thin when heated.)

1 13-OUNCE CAN COCONUT MILK

2 OUNCES RED CURRY PASTE

¾ CUP UNSWEETENED PEANUT BUTTER

½ TABLESPOON SALT

½ CUP SUGAR

2 TABLESPOONS APPLE CIDER VINEGAR

½ CUP WATER

¼ TEASPOON SPICY RED PEPPER FLAKES

1 TEASPOON TOASTED SESAME OIL

TOASTED PEANUT SAUCE

Clarified Butter

1. Place a skillet over the lowest heat possible. Cut the butter into smaller chunks and sprinkle it over the bottom of the skillet. Do not stir.

2. The butter will separate into three layers as it melts. The top layer is foam. Use a large spoon to skim it off slowly and discard.

3. Let the butter cook for about 10 minutes, skimming as necessary.

4. Place two plain paper towels in a fine mesh strainer. Over a heatproof container, slowly pour the butter through the towels to remove the remaining foam. Stop pouring before the brown milk solids can make it into the dish. Put a tight lid on the container and store in the refrigerator.

1¼ CUPS UNSALTED BUTTER

Mango Chutney

1. Place a large enameled skillet or enameled Dutch oven over medium heat. Add the sugar and vinegar and stir continually until the sugar dissolves. Lower the heat to the lowest setting.

2. Add the remaining ingredients and simmer uncovered for 45 minutes. It should be syrupy and thick.

3. Pour into a clean, airtight jar and store in the refrigerator for up to 1 month.

1 CUP SUGAR

½ CUP APPLE CIDER VINEGAR

3 FRESH MANGOES, PEELED AND CHOPPED IN ¾" PIECES

1 SMALL ONION, CHOPPED

¼ CUP GOLDEN RAISINS OR CHOPPED DATES

1 GARLIC CLOVE, MINCED

½ TEASPOON WHOLE MUSTARD SEEDS

½ TEASPOON RED CHILI FLAKES

Fig Balsamic Dessert Sauce

1. Place a skillet over medium heat. Once it is heated, place everything but the vinegar in the skillet and bring to a boil. Lower the heat to medium-low and simmer for 10–15 minutes. It should be frothy and reduced by half.

2. Add the vinegar and increase the heat to medium-high. Stir frequently for 5 minutes. The sauce is ready when it sticks to the back of the spoon.

3. Use a stand or stick blender to purée the sauce. Serve hot or warm. Refrigerate any leftovers for 2 weeks.

8 DRIED FIGS, STEMMED AND MINCED

2 CUPS APPLE JUICE

¼ CUP SUGAR

¼ CUP BALSAMIC VINEGAR

Vietnamese Chili Garlic Sauce

1. Place all of the ingredients in a blender or food processor. Pulse until the mixture is smooth. Add 1–2 tablespoons of water if necessary.

2. Place a skillet over medium heat. Once it is heated, pour the mixture into the skillet and bring to a simmer.

3. Reduce the heat to low and simmer uncovered for 10 minutes. It should lose its raw smell and develop a richer smell. Transfer to an airtight jar.

6 OUNCES THAI, SERRANO, CAYENNE, OR RED JALAPEÑO PEPPERS

4 GARLIC CLOVES, CHOPPED

1 TEASPOON SALT

2 TEASPOONS HONEY

2 TABLESPOONS APPLE CIDER VINEGAR OR RICE WINE VINEGAR

1–2 TABLESPOONS WATER (OPTIONAL)

Caramelized Onion and Fennel

1. Cut off the green part of the fennel and the base. Discard. Separate the pieces and rinse well to remove any dirt. Slice thinly.

2. Place a Dutch oven over medium heat. Once it is warmed, add the olive oil and the vegetables. Sprinkle the salt across the top and stir to combine. Cover the pan with a lid and reduce the heat to low. Stir the vegetables every 3 minutes, three times.

3. Add a little more oil if the pan seems dry and let it cook for about an hour, stirring every 15 minutes. The mixture should be very juicy. Turn the heat to high and stir frequently for 5 minutes, or until the liquid evaporates.

2 HEADS FENNEL

2 TABLESPOONS OLIVE OIL

2 LARGE SWEET ONIONS, PEELED AND THINLY SLICED

2 SMALL TOMATOES, CORED AND SLICED

1 TEASPOON SALT

Green Curry Paste

YIELDS ½ CUP

1. Remove the bottom 3" from the lemongrass and the dried fibrous tops. Cut into 1" pieces. Add to a food processor with the ginger, cilantro, peppers, onion, garlic, and lime zest. Pulse for several minutes until it is a smooth paste.

2. Add the coriander, cumin, honey, soy sauce, and oil and pulse until it is combined.

3. Place a skillet over medium heat. Add the curry paste, spreading it out evenly. Cook for 7–10 minutes, stirring frequently, until the pepper smell is overpowering. If the mixture sticks, add a tablespoon of oil.

4. Once the paste is ready, remove from the skillet. Store refrigerated for 2 weeks or frozen for up to 6 months.

2 STALKS LEMONGRASS

2" PIECE GINGER, PEELED AND SLICED

½ BUNCH CILANTRO

4 JALAPEÑOS, SEEDED

1 SMALL YELLOW ONION, PEELED AND QUARTERED

3 GARLIC CLOVES, PEELED

ZEST FROM 1 LIME

1 TEASPOON GROUND CORIANDER

1 TABLESPOON GROUND CUMIN

1 TEASPOON HONEY

1 TABLESPOON SOY SAUCE

3 TABLESPOONS PEANUT OIL

Bolognese Sauce

1. Place a Dutch oven over medium heat and add the butter and oil. Once the butter has melted, add the onion, stirring continually for 1 minute until slightly translucent. Stir in the celery and carrot and cook for 2 minutes.

2. Add the ground beef and stir continually, breaking the meat into small pieces while it cooks. Once the meat is slightly more brown than red, turn the heat up to medium-high and add the wine. Leave uncovered and simmering vigorously. Stir occasionally for 10 minutes to prevent it from sticking while the wine evaporates.

3. Add the milk and the nutmeg and lower the heat to medium. Stir continually until it stops boiling vigorously. Continue to stir it frequently for about 6–8 minutes until the milk evaporates. Add the tomatoes and reduce the heat to low. You want it to bubble occasionally but barely simmer.

4. Cooking time will vary between 3½ and 5 hours. Once all of the liquid has evaporated, you'll be left with a meaty, gravy-like sauce. Taste and add salt if necessary.

3 TABLESPOONS BUTTER

3 TABLESPOONS OLIVE OIL

½ SMALL YELLOW ONION, CHOPPED

½ CELERY STALK, CHOPPED

½ CARROT, CHOPPED

¾ POUND LEAN GROUND BEEF

1 CUP DRY WHITE WINE

½ CUP WHOLE MILK

⅛ TEASPOON GROUND NUTMEG

1 28-OUNCE CAN CHOPPED ITALIAN TOMATOES

1 TEASPOON SALT, AS DESIRED

Ethiopian Berberé Red Pepper Paste

YIELDS 1½ CUPS

1. Place a dry cast-iron skillet over medium heat. Once it is hot, add the ginger, cardamom, coriander, nutmeg, cloves, allspice, and cinnamon and cook for 1 minute. They should start to smell nutty.

2. Pour the spices into a blender and add the onion, garlic, salt, and ¼ cup of water. Blend into a paste.

3. Reduce the heat on the skillet to low. Add the paprika, cayenne pepper, and black pepper in the skillet. Toast for 1–2 minutes. Stir in the rest of the water, ¼ cup at a time. Once the water is combined, stir in the blended mixture.

4. Stir continuously for 10–15 minutes. Transfer the paste to a jar and cool to room temperature. Store in the refrigerator for several weeks, as long as there is a film of oil on top of the paste.

1 TEASPOON GROUND GINGER

1 TEASPOON GROUND CARDAMOM

1 TEASPOON GROUND CORIANDER

¼ TEASPOON GROUND NUTMEG

⅛ TEASPOON GROUND CLOVES

⅛ TEASPOON GROUND ALLSPICE

½ TEASPOON GROUND CINNAMON

2 TABLESPOONS ONION, MINCED

2 GARLIC CLOVES, MINCED

2 TABLESPOONS SALT

1½ CUPS WATER

1 CUP SWEET PAPRIKA

½ CUP SMOKY PAPRIKA

2 TEASPOONS GROUND CAYENNE PEPPER

½ TEASPOON BLACK PEPPER

Roasted Tomatillo and Green Chili Sauce

YIELDS 1 PINT

1. Preheat oven to 350°F. Remove the papery husks from the tomatillos and wash them. Remove the core and cut into quarters.

2. Place a large skillet over medium heat and once it is heated, add the olive oil, tomatillos, onion, garlic, and chilies. Shake the pan frequently to keep ingredients from sticking. Cook for about 10 minutes. Place the skillet in the middle of the oven.

3. Roast for 30 minutes. Remove the pan from the oven and cool.

4. Place the vegetables in a blender or food processor. Add the lime juice. Pulse several times to get the desired texture. Taste and add salt as needed. Place in a tightly sealed container and refrigerate for up to one week.

10 TOMATILLOS

1 TABLESPOON OLIVE OIL

1 SMALL ONION, QUARTERED

2 CLOVES GARLIC, PEELED

2 ANAHEIM CHILIES, SEEDED

JUICE FROM 2 LIMES

SALT TO TASTE

Onion Marmalade

YIELDS 1 PINT

1. Place a Dutch oven over low heat. Once it's warm, add the olive oil and stir in the onions with the salt and bay leaf. Cover and cook for 15 minutes.

2. Stir it a few times to prevent sticking. Once the onions are translucent, remove the lid. Add the sherry and stir. Let the liquid evaporate and stir every few minutes to prevent burning.

3. Replace the lid and cook for 1–1½ hours. If more liquid accumulates, remove the lid and let the liquid evaporate. Once there is no liquid in the pan and the onions are a light golden color, remove the bay leaf, and the marmalade is ready to serve.

2 TABLESPOONS OLIVE OIL

2 LARGE WHITE OR YELLOW ONIONS, THINLY SLICED

½ TEASPOON SALT

1 BAY LEAF

¼ CUP SHERRY, BRANDY, OR A SWEET WHITE WINE

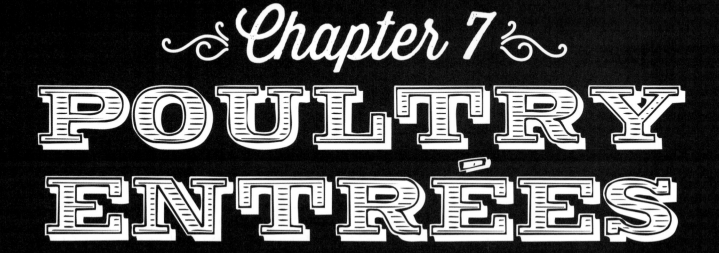

Chapter 7
POULTRY ENTRÉES

Rustic Turkey Burger with Mushrooms and Zucchini

YIELDS 4 SERVINGS

1. Place a skillet over medium heat. Once it is heated, add 1 teaspoon vegetable oil and the onion. Cook for 3–4 minutes, or until very soft. Remove the skillet from the heat and put the onion in a large bowl. Combine all other ingredients, except for the turkey and remaining teaspoon of vegetable oil, and stir until well combined.

2. Break the turkey up over the surface of the bowl. Use your hands to gently massage the meat into the other ingredients. Combine the meat into four equally shaped balls.

3. Flatten balls into patties and then wrap them in plastic wrap. Place in the refrigerator to rest for at least 20 minutes.

4. Place a skillet over medium heat and add 1 teaspoon of vegetable oil. Place two patties into the skillet and cook for 4–5 minutes or until well browned.

5. Flip patties, cover the skillet with a lid, and let cook for an additional 4–5 minutes. Check the center to make sure they're cooked through. Repeat for remaining two patties.

2 TEASPOONS VEGETABLE OIL

½ CUP SHREDDED ONION

¾ CUP BREAD CRUMBS

1 TEASPOON SOY SAUCE

1 TEASPOON WORCESTERSHIRE SAUCE

½ TEASPOON GARLIC POWDER

¼ TEASPOON GROUND MUSTARD

¼ TEASPOON GROUND BLACK PEPPER

1 TEASPOON SALT

¼ CUP SHREDDED ZUCCHINI

¼ CUP MUSHROOMS, MINCED

1 POUND GROUND TURKEY

Pan-Roasted Turkey Wings

YIELDS 4 SERVINGS

1. Preheat oven to 300°F. Place a rack in the middle of the oven.

2. Sprinkle the wing pieces lightly with salt. Place a skillet over medium heat. Once it is heated, add the oil and the wings to the skillet. Cook on each side for 3 minutes, or until they're lightly browned.

3. Whisk the ketchup, apple juice, Tabasco sauce, onion, garlic, and thyme in a small bowl. Pour the sauce over the wings and place the pan in the middle of the oven.

4. Cook for 30 minutes. Use tongs to turn them over and continue cooking them for another 15–20 minutes, or until the meat is tender and the sauce has thickened.

5. Serve the sauce in a small bowl alongside the wings.

8 TURKEY WINGS, TIPS REMOVED AND SECTIONS SEPARATED

1 TEASPOON SALT

2 TABLESPOONS OLIVE OIL

3 CUPS KETCHUP

3 CUPS APPLE JUICE

2 TEASPOONS TABASCO SAUCE

1 LARGE ONION, CHOPPED

8 GARLIC CLOVES, SMASHED

2 TEASPOONS FRESH THYME LEAVES

Braised and Pan-Seared Duck Legs

YIELDS 2 SERVINGS

1. Sprinkle the duck legs with salt and pepper. Place in an air-tight container with bay leaves and thyme and refrigerate for 12–24 hours.

2. Place a skillet over medium-low heat. Once it is heated, add the skin to the skillet and cook for 1 hour, stirring occasionally to keep the fat from sticking. Cool for 15 minutes.

3. Preheat oven to 300°F. Carefully place the duck legs in the skillet with the bay leaves and thyme. Place in the middle of the oven and cook for 2 hours, or until the bone moves independently of the meat. The skin should be crispy.

4. Remove the pan from the oven and set it aside to cool. Let the oil cool and pour off the fat. Note: Duck fat will keep for up to 2 months in an airtight container in the refrigerator.

2 DUCK LEGS WITH SKIN ON

SALT TO TASTE

PEPPER TO TASTE

2 BAY LEAVES, CRUMBLED

THUMB-SIZED BUNDLE OF FRESH THYME

SKIN FROM REMAINDER OF DUCK

Turkey Fillets with Anchovies, Capers, and Dill

YIELDS 4 SERVINGS

1. Place a skillet over medium heat. Once the skillet is heated, add the oil and the anchovies. Cook for 5 minutes, stirring continually, or until they fall apart.

2. Place as many turkey fillets in the skillet as possible without overlapping. Cook on each side for 3 minutes, or until they're nicely browned. Repeat as necessary and remove the cooked fillets to a plate and keep warm.

3. Add the chicken broth to the pan and use a spoon to scrape up any bits from the bottom of the pan. Stir in the capers. Cook for 1 minute until the sauce reduces.

4. Pour the sauce over the turkey fillets and sprinkle them with chopped dill. Serve while warm.

2 TABLESPOONS OLIVE OIL

6 ANCHOVY FILLETS OR 1 TABLESPOON ANCHOVY PASTE

4 TURKEY FILLETS, 4-6 OUNCES EACH, POUNDED THIN

¼ CUP CHICKEN BROTH

1 TABLESPOON CAPERS, CHOPPED

2 TABLESPOONS DILL, CHOPPED

Ginger Chicken

1. Rinse the chicken breasts and pat dry. Mix the flour with the ground ginger, salt, and pepper. Dredge the chicken in the flour and shake to remove excess flour.

2. Place a skillet over medium heat. Once it is warmed, add the oil and the chicken breasts. Cook on each side for 2–3 minutes. Remove from the pan and set aside.

3. Stir the remaining ingredients in a bowl and pour into the hot skillet. Once the mixture starts to boil, lower the heat to medium-low and return the chicken to the pan. Cook on each side for 12 minutes.

4. Once the center of the chicken is no longer pink, remove it from the skillet and serve over rice.

4 BONELESS, SKINLESS CHICKEN BREASTS

1 CUP FLOUR

2 TEASPOONS GROUND GINGER

1 TEASPOON SALT

½ TEASPOON GROUND BLACK PEPPER

3 TABLESPOONS VEGETABLE OIL

¼ CUP SOY SAUCE

¾ CUP BROWN SUGAR

1 20-OUNCE CAN CRUSHED PINEAPPLE, DRAINED

½ CUP WATER

Pressed and Roasted Cornish Game Hens

YIELDS 4 SERVINGS

1. Preheat oven to 400°F. Place two cast-iron skillets in the middle rack of the oven. One skillet must be able to fit inside the other and the skillet that will be on top must be large enough to cover both hens.

2. Rinse the hens. Cut the spines off the bird to they can be flattened out. If necessary, snip the breast bone to permit the bird to flatten. Pat the birds dry and sprinkle both sides lightly with salt and pepper.

3. Mix the minced herbs into the softened butter. Slide your fingers between the skin and the meat of the chicken. Rub the butter under the skin and on top of each bird evenly.

4. Remove the bottom skillet from the oven, place the birds skin-side down, and cook over medium-high heat for 3–4 minutes. Flip them and place in the middle of the oven with the other skillet on top. Cook for 25 minutes, or until the internal temperature of the breast is 160°F. Place the birds on a plate, cover loosely with foil, and set aside to rest.

5. Place the skillet that held the chicken over medium-high heat. Let most of the liquid boil off, but stir to remove any bits stuck to the pan. Once the liquid in the skillet turns light brown, add the shallot and cook for 2–3 minutes. Add the stock to the skillet and stir vigorously. Once the liquid has evaporated, turn off the heat.

6. Cut each chicken in half. Place each half on a plate and spoon out some of the shallot and pan sauce over the chicken. Serve immediately.

2 ROCK CORNISH HENS

SALT AND PEPPER TO TASTE

SMALL HANDFUL OF FRESH OREGANO, TARRAGON, OR THYME LEAVES, MINCED

3 TABLESPOONS SOFTENED BUTTER

1 SHALLOT, MINCED

¼ CUP VEGETABLE OR CHICKEN STOCK

Apricot-Stuffed Chicken Thighs

YIELDS 4 SERVINGS

1. Place a skillet over medium-high heat. Once it is heated, add the oil and onion and cook for 10–12 minutes. Remove half of the onion mixture from the skillet and put into a bowl.

2. Add the carrot and celery to the skillet and cook for 4–5 minutes, or until the celery is just starting to soften. Turn off the heat.

3. Trim any excess fat from the thighs and lightly pound them so they're flat. Add the apricot, cheese, panko, thyme, and a sprinkle of salt and pepper to the bowl. Toss lightly and add ¼ of the mixture to each thigh.

4. Roll the thigh starting with the widest edge and rolling toward the smallest edge. Use toothpicks or kitchen twine to hold it together. Place it back in the skillet over medium-high heat. Move the vegetables to the edges of the skillet. Sear the chicken on each side for 3–4 minutes, or until it is lightly browned on all sides.

5. Reduce the heat to medium-low, cover, and cook for 20 minutes, until the center measures 150°F. Turn off the heat and let it rest for 5 minutes before serving.

2 TABLESPOONS OLIVE OIL

1 LARGE ONION, THINLY SLICED

1 CARROT, THINLY SLICED

1 STALK CELERY, THINLY SLICED

4 BONELESS, SKINLESS CHICKEN THIGHS

½ CUP DRIED APRICOTS, CHOPPED

½ CUP PROVOLONE CHEESE, CUBED

¾ CUP PANKO OR UNSEASONED BREAD CRUMBS

1 TABLESPOON CHOPPED FRESH THYME

PINCH SALT

PINCH PEPPER

Bourbon-Glazed Chicken

YIELDS 4 SERVINGS

1. Place a skillet over medium heat. Once it is heated, add the oil, carrots, celery, and onion and cook for 5–7 minutes, stirring frequently. The vegetables should be soft and the onions should be turning brown.

2. Pour the chicken broth over the vegetables. Sprinkle the breasts with salt and pepper and place on top of the vegetables. Cover the skillet and steam for about15 minutes.

3. Remove the lid and place the chicken on a plate and keep warm. Increase the heat and add the bourbon. Let the liquid boil for 10–15 minutes, or until it becomes very thick.

4. Return the chicken breasts to the pan with the almond slivers. Cook the chicken for 2 minutes on each side to warm and become coated in sauce.

5. Place a ½ cup of rice in the middle of a plate with a chicken breast on top. Spoon the vegetables and glaze over the chicken. Serve while hot.

2 TABLESPOONS VEGETABLE OIL

2 CARROTS, GRATED

1 STALK CELERY, THINLY SLICED

1 SMALL YELLOW ONION, DICED

¼ CUP CHICKEN BROTH

4 BONELESS, SKINLESS CHICKEN BREASTS

PINCH SALT

PINCH PEPPER

2 TABLESPOONS BOURBON

2 CUPS COOKED WHITE RICE

¼ CUP ALMOND SLIVERS

Sesame Chicken Stir-Fry

YIELDS 4 SERVINGS

1. Mix the scallion, garlic, ginger, soy sauce, honey, cornstarch, 1 teaspoon of the salt, sherry, and sesame oil in a bowl. Stir to eliminate all lumps of cornstarch. Add the chicken, toss to coat, and let the bowl sit at room temperature for 15–30 minutes.

2. Cut broccoli florets into bite-sized pieces. Slice the stalks into pieces about ¼" thick and no more than 2" long. Place a large skillet over high heat. Add 1 tablespoon of the oil along with the broccoli stems. Stir frequently for 30 seconds. Add the florets and 2 tablespoons of water. Toss and cook for 2 minutes before transferring to a bowl.

3. Add the remaining 2 tablespoons of oil. Remove the chicken from the marinade and add to the skillet. Toss continually for 3 minutes, or until the chicken starts to turn brown. Add the hoisin sauce and the broccoli and toss to combine. Add the marinade and stir continually until the sauce thickens.

4. Taste and season with salt and pepper before serving over cooked white rice. Sprinkle toasted sesame seeds over the dish.

3 SCALLIONS, THINLY SLICED

2 CLOVES GARLIC, MINCED

1" PIECE GINGER, PEELED AND THINLY SLICED

1 TABLESPOON SOY SAUCE

1 TABLESPOON HONEY

1 TABLESPOON CORNSTARCH

1¼ TEASPOONS SALT

1 TABLESPOON SHERRY

1 TABLESPOON SESAME OIL

1 POUND BONELESS, SKINLESS CHICKEN BREAST, CUT INTO CUBES

1 BROCCOLI HEAD

3 TABLESPOONS VEGETABLE OIL

2 TABLESPOONS COLD WATER

1 TABLESPOON HOISIN SAUCE

1 TABLESPOON TOASTED SESAME SEEDS

DATE AND BALSAMIC-MARINATED CHICKEN BREAST

Date and Balsamic–Marinated Chicken Breast

YIELDS 4 SERVINGS

1. Remove the pits from the dates and chop finely. Place them in a bowl with all of the other ingredients except the chicken and oil. Microwave in 20-second increments while stirring until the honey and vinegar can be easily combined. Pat the chicken breasts dry and place them in the marinade. Cover the bowl and let it sit on the counter for 30–60 minutes.

2. Place a grill pan over medium-high heat and add 2 tablespoons of oil. Remove each breast from the marinade and let the excess marinade drip off. Once the oil is hot, add the chicken to the skillet so the pieces don't touch. (Cook in batches if necessary.) Cook the first side for about 3 minutes. Turn and cook the second side for 3 minutes.

3. Reduce the heat to medium and cook until the center is no longer pink. Remove the breasts from the pan and let them rest. Pour the remaining marinade into the grill pan and bring to a boil before pouring over the breasts.

1 CUP DRIED DATES (ABOUT 12)

½ CUP HONEY

½ CUP BALSAMIC VINEGAR

½ TEASPOON SALT

½ TEASPOON HUNGARIAN PAPRIKA

1 CUP FLOUR

4 BONELESS, SKINLESS CHICKEN BREASTS

3 TABLESPOONS VEGETABLE OIL

Chicken Étouffée

1. Season the chicken with salt and pepper and coat them with flour. Heat a skillet over medium-high heat. Add the oil. Once the oil is heated, add the chicken and cook for 7 minutes on the first side. Flip the chicken and cook for 6–7 minutes more. Don't crowd the chicken; cook it in batches. Place the cooked chicken on a plate and keep it warm.

2. Stir the remaining flour into the pan to make a light roux. Add the onions, peppers, and garlic.

3. Reduce the heat to low and stir in the thyme and the sage. Add the broth, slowly whisking the flour mixture to prevent lumps. Once you have a smooth sauce, return the chicken to the pot and bring to a boil.

4. Reduce the heat to low, cover, and cook for 20 minutes. The chicken should be very tender. Stir and flip occasionally.

5. Skim off any fat that may come to the top. Serve it over bowls of hot rice with hot sauce to taste.

1½ POUNDS BONE-IN CHICKEN THIGHS

PINCH SALT

PINCH PEPPER

½ CUP ALL-PURPOSE FLOUR

½ CUP VEGETABLE OIL

2 MEDIUM ONIONS, CHOPPED

2 MEDIUM BELL PEPPERS, CHOPPED

2 JALAPEÑO PEPPERS, SEEDED, STEMMED, AND MINCED

15 GARLIC CLOVES, PEELED AND MINCED

2 TEASPOONS DRIED THYME

2 TEASPOONS DRIED SAGE

3 CUPS CHICKEN BROTH

½ CUP COOKED WHITE RICE PER SERVING

HOT SAUCE TO TASTE

Coconut and Basil Chicken

YIELDS 4 SERVINGS

1. Combine the scallion, ginger, coconut milk, basil, garlic, honey, and fish sauce in a blender and purée until smooth.

2. Remove any fat or skin from the chicken, cut the meat into 1" cubes, and sprinkle the chicken with a little salt and pepper.

3. Place a skillet over medium-high heat. When it is warm, add the vegetable oil. Add the chicken. Cook for 3 minutes on each side or until lightly browned. Reduce heat to medium-low.

4. Pour the coconut sauce and jalapeños over the chicken. Cover and cook for 8–10 minutes until the sauce just starts to bubble. Once the chicken is firm and no longer pink in the middle, it is ready to serve with the garnishes over cooked rice.

1 SCALLION, CHOPPED WITH WHITE AND GREEN SEPARATED

2" PIECE GINGER, PEELED AND CUT INTO MATCHSTICKS

1 CUP COCONUT MILK

1 CUP THAI BASIL LEAVES

3 GARLIC CLOVES

2 TEASPOONS HONEY

1 TEASPOON FISH SAUCE

½ POUND BONELESS, SKINLESS CHICKEN BREAST OR THIGHS

SALT TO TASTE

PEPPER TO TASTE

1 TABLESPOON VEGETABLE OIL

1 JALAPEÑO PEPPER, SEEDED AND THINLY SLICED

½ CUP CHOPPED CILANTRO, FOR GARNISH

2 TABLESPOONS TOASTED COCONUT FOR GARNISH

2 LIME SLICES FOR GARNISH

4 CUPS COOKED WHITE JASMINE RICE

Chicken Asapao

1. *For Sofrito:* Place all ingredients in a food processor and pulse until well blended. Leftovers can be frozen.

2. *For Chicken Asapao:* Place a Dutch oven over medium heat. Once it is heated, add the chicken breasts and the chicken broth. Add water if necessary so the breasts are covered. Cook for 30 minutes. Remove the breasts from the pan and cut into ¼" cubes.

3. Return the chicken cubes to the pan with everything except the lime. Stir to combine. Reduce the heat to low and cover. Simmer for 45–60 minutes, or until the chicken is soft.

4. Remove the bay leaves and stir the lime juice into the pan. Serve it over rice with a sprinkle of freshly chopped cilantro and hot sauce if desired.

SOFRITO

1 LARGE ONION, PEELED AND CUT INTO QUARTERS

3 CUBANELLE PEPPERS, STEMS AND SEEDS REMOVED

3 GARLIC CLOVES

½ BUNCH CILANTRO

3 TOMATOES, STEMS REMOVED

1 GREEN BELL PEPPER, STEM AND SEEDS REMOVED

CHICKEN ASAPAO

1 POUND BONELESS, SKINLESS CHICKEN BREASTS

3 CUPS CHICKEN BROTH

2 MEDIUM POTATOES

1 8-OUNCE CAN TOMATO SAUCE

¼ CUP SOFRITO

1 TEASPOON SALT

2 BAY LEAVES

¼ CUP SMALL GREEN OLIVES

JUICE FROM 1 LIME

Malaysian Turmeric and Honey Chicken

YIELDS 4 SERVINGS

1. Rinse the chicken breasts and remove any excess fat.

2. Combine all of the remaining ingredients except for the oil and honey in a large plastic bag. Nestle the chicken into the marinade and let it rest in the refrigerator for 4–12 hours before cooking.

3. Remove the chicken and shallots from the marinade. Place a skillet over medium heat. Once it is heated, add the oil to the skillet and several pieces of the chicken, being sure not to crowd. Cook for 5 minutes before rotating a quarter turn. Repeat until the chicken is cooked through. Remove to a platter and keep warm.

4. Place the shallots in the skillet and cook for 5–7 minutes. Add the marinade into the skillet, deglazing the pan. Simmer for 10 minutes, or until the marinade is reduced by half. Add the honey and stir until combined. Return the chicken to the pan, tossing until it is well coated. Serve with white rice.

4 BONELESS, SKINLESS CHICKEN BREASTS

1 BOTTLE GINGER ALE OR BEER

JUICE FROM 2 LIMES

3" SECTION OF GINGER, PEELED AND GRATED

1 TEASPOON GROUND TURMERIC

½ TEASPOON SALT

2 TEASPOONS GROUND CINNAMON

1 TEASPOON GROUND CARDAMOM

2 GARLIC CLOVES, MINCED

3 SHALLOTS, SLICED

1 SERRANO OR FINGER PEPPER, THINLY SLICED

2 TABLESPOONS PEANUT OR VEGETABLE OIL

2 TABLESPOONS HONEY

Picante Chicken and Black Beans Pasta in an Ancho Chili Sauce

YIELDS 4 SERVINGS

1. Place a large pot of water over high heat to boil. Once it comes to a boil, add the pasta and cook according to the package directions.

2. Cover the chilies with hot water for 30 minutes to soften. Remove them from the water and finely chop. Reserve the water.

3. Place a skillet over medium-high heat. Once it is heated, add the oil, chilies, onion, bell pepper, and chicken. Cook for 4–5 minutes. Add the tomatoes, cumin, chicken broth, and 1 cup of the water the chilies soaked in. Stir to combine.

4. Once the chicken is cooked through, add the beans and bring to a simmer. Divide the cooked pasta in equal portions into 4 bowls. Pour the chicken and sauce over the pasta and serve immediately.

WATER, AS NEEDED

1 POUND WHOLE-WHEAT FARFALLE

2 DRIED ANCHO CHILIES, STEMMED AND SEEDED

1 TABLESPOON OLIVE OIL

½ SMALL ONION, CHOPPED

½ YELLOW BELL PEPPER, CHOPPED

½ POUND CHICKEN BREAST TENDERLOINS, CUBED

2 SMALL TOMATOES, CHOPPED

¼ TEASPOON GROUND CUMIN

1 CUP CHICKEN BROTH

1 CAN BLACK BEANS, DRAINED AND RINSED

Seared and Baked Duck Breasts with Fruit Compote

YIELDS 2 SERVINGS

1. *For Savory Fruit Compote:* Place shallot in a hot skillet with duck fat. Cook for 3 minutes. Stir in fruit jam, sherry, and balsamic vinegar. Cook for 1 minute; set aside.

2. *For Seared and Baked Duck Breasts:* Place the water, salt, and sugar in a small saucepan over medium heat. Stir until the salt and sugar have dissolved. Transfer to a large sealable container. Place the duck breasts on a cutting board and drag a knife across the skin in diagonal lines that are 1" apart. Rotate the breast and cut again to create a diamond pattern. Place the duck in the brine in the refrigerator. Let it rest for at least 8 (but no more than 24) hours.

3. Preheat oven to 400°F. Heat a skillet over medium heat. Remove the duck from the brine and pat dry. Place the breasts skin-side down in the skillet and cook for 1 minute. Nudge the breasts to loosen them if necessary and cook for 5 more minutes.

4. Turn off the heat and drain the fat. Flip the breasts over so they're skin-side up and place skillet in the middle of the oven for 5 minutes.

5. Remove from the oven. Cover the skillet with a lid and let sit for 4 minutes. Remove the breasts from the pan and place on a plate loosely covered with foil for 5 minutes. Reheat compote until warm.

6. Cut the breasts in ½"-thick slices on an angle. Fan out on a plate before pouring compote over them to serve.

SAVORY FRUIT COMPOTE

1 SHALLOT, MINCED

2 TABLESPOONS DUCK FAT

½ CUP FRUIT JAM

¼ CUP SHERRY

2 TABLESPOONS BALSAMIC VINEGAR

SEARED AND BAKED DUCK BREASTS

1 QUART WARM WATER

¼ CUP TABLE SALT

2 TABLESPOONS SUGAR

2 BONELESS, SKIN-ON DUCK BREASTS

SAVORY FRUIT COMPOTE, AS DESIRED

Spicy Cumin and Chili Turkey Breast

1. Rinse the turkey breast. If desired, remove the skin and bones before cooking. Pat the breast dry.

2. Combine all of the spices in a small bowl and stir to combine. Rub the spice mix over the meat. Place it in a sealable container and store in the refrigerator for 4–24 hours.

3. Preheat oven to 325°F. Place a skillet over medium-high heat. Add the oil and the turkey breast. Cook on each side for 4–5 minutes, or until it is lightly seared.

4. Place the pan in the center of the oven and cook uncovered for 1½ hours, or until a meat thermometer registers 155°F. Remove the meat from the pan, cover, and let it rest for 10 minutes.

5. Add the stock to the pan and scrape to remove any stuck-on bits from the bottom of the pan. Add the flour, whisking continually for several minutes. Place the pan over medium heat and cook until thickened. Slice the turkey and serve the pan sauce over the slices while warm.

1 4- OR 5-POUND TURKEY BREAST

3 TABLESPOONS GROUND CUMIN

1 TEASPOON TABLE SALT

½ TEASPOON GROUND BLACK PEPPER

½ TEASPOON CHILI POWDER

1 TEASPOON GARLIC POWDER

1 TEASPOON ONION POWDER

2 TABLESPOONS OLIVE OIL

½ CUP CHICKEN OR TURKEY STOCK

2 TABLESPOONS FLOUR

SPICY CUMIN AND CHILI TURKEY BREAST

Grilled Turkey Cutlets with Honey and Mango

1. Place a small skillet or saucepan over medium heat. Combine the juice, honey, Tabasco, salt, and black pepper and bring to a boil. Boil for 10–15 minutes until the sauce is reduced and thickened slightly.

2. Place a grill pan over medium-high heat and lightly grease the ridges. Spoon the sauce over the cutlets and sprinkle with salt and pepper. Place the cutlets on the grill pan and cook each side for 2–3 minutes.

3. Dip the mango slices in the fruit sauce and place on the grill pan. Cook on each side until there are grill marks. Serve the turkey and fruit over rice or noodles. Pour the leftover sauce on each serving.

½ CUP POMEGRANATE JUICE

2 TABLESPOONS HONEY

SEVERAL DASHES TABASCO SAUCE

½ TEASPOON SALT PLUS MORE TO TASTE

¼ TEASPOON BLACK PEPPER PLUS MORE TO TASTE

4 THIN-CUT TURKEY CUTLETS (1¼ POUNDS)

VEGETABLE OIL, AS NEEDED

2 LARGE FRESH MANGOES, PEELED AND SLICED ½" THICK

Deviled Chicken

1. Preheat oven to 425°F. Place a skillet over medium-high heat. When the pan is hot, add the oil and onion. Stir frequently and cook for 5–7 minutes. Combine the mustard and spices in a bowl.

2. Remove the skin from the chicken, rinse, and pat dry. Place the chicken on top of the onion and sear each side for 3–4 minutes. While flipping, stir the onions to prevent them from burning. Once the exterior is seared, brush the mustard mixture over the chicken.

3. Cook, covered, in the middle of the oven for 30–35 minutes. The chicken is done when the internal temperature of the meat is 160°F. Sprinkle lightly with paprika to garnish and serve immediately.

1 TABLESPOON OLIVE OIL

1 SMALL ONION, PEELED AND CHOPPED

¼ CUP MUSTARD

1 TEASPOON HUNGARIAN PAPRIKA

½ TEASPOON PEPPER

½ TEASPOON SALT

1 POUND CHICKEN THIGHS

Coconut Milk Fried Chicken

1. Combine the spices, sugar, salt, and shallots in a food processor and pulse until the mixture resembles creamy mashed potatoes. Add the coconut milk and pulse till combined. Rinse the chicken pieces and trim any fat. Place the chicken into a glass bowl and cover with the coconut milk mixture. Cover and refrigerate for 3 hours or overnight.

2. Remove the chicken pieces from the milk mixture and pat dry. Cover and let sit at room temperature for 30 minutes. Place 1" of oil in a chicken fryer or Dutch oven on medium or medium-high heat. The oil should measure 375°F but shouldn't smoke.

3. Place two to three pieces of the chicken in the oil at a time. Fry for 10 minutes on each side. Larger pieces of dark meat may need to be fried up to 12 minutes on each side. Serve warm.

1 TABLESPOON GROUND CINNAMON

1 TABLESPOON CHILI POWDER

1 TABLESPOON GROUND CORIANDER

1 TEASPOON GROUND CUMIN

1 TEASPOON BLACK PEPPER

2 TEASPOONS GROUND TURMERIC

2 TEASPOONS SUGAR

1 TEASPOON SALT

5 SHALLOTS, COARSELY CHOPPED

1 CAN COCONUT MILK

3 POUNDS CHICKEN PARTS

2-3 CUPS PEANUT OIL FOR FRYING

Moroccan Chicken Tagine

1. Combine half of the garlic with the spices and set aside. Combine the other half of the garlic with half of the lemon zest and set aside. Pat the chicken dry and season with salt and pepper.

2. Place a pan over medium-high heat. Add the oil and chicken. Brown on each side for 6 minutes. Cook the chicken in batches if necessary to prevent the chicken from touching. Remove the chicken and set aside.

3. Pour off all but 1 tablespoon of the fat and add the onion and remaining lemon zest. Reduce the heat to medium and cook while stirring occasionally for 5–7 minutes. Add the garlic and spice mixture and cook for 1 minute, stirring continually. Stir in the carrots, broth, and honey and scrape the bottom of the pan. Return the chicken to the pan, keeping everything on a single layer. Cover, reduce the heat to medium-low, and simmer 1 hour.

4. Transfer the chicken to a serving platter and tent with foil. Skim off the fat from the sauce, add the olives, and increase the heat to medium. Boil for 5–7 minutes. The sauce should thicken slightly, the carrots should be tender, and the olives warm. Stir in the garlic and lemon zest mixture, the cilantro, and the lemon juice and return the chicken to the pan, coating it in sauce. Serve with couscous or rice.

6 GARLIC CLOVES, MINCED AND DIVIDED

1½ TEASPOONS SWEET PAPRIKA

½ TEASPOON CUMIN

½ TEASPOON CORIANDER

½ TEASPOON CINNAMON

¼ TEASPOON GROUND GINGER

⅛ TEASPOON CAYENNE PEPPER

1 TEASPOON MINCED LEMON ZEST

4 POUNDS CHICKEN THIGHS

SALT TO TASTE

PEPPER TO TASTE

2 TABLESPOONS OLIVE OIL

1 LARGE ONION, CUT INTO ¼" WEDGES

2 LARGE CARROTS, PEELED AND CUT INTO ½" ROUNDS

2 CUPS CHICKEN BROTH

1 TABLESPOON HONEY

1 CUP PITTED GREEN OLIVES

3 TABLESPOONS CHOPPED CILANTRO

JUICE FROM 2 LEMONS

COQ AU VIN

Coq Au Vin

YIELDS 4–5 SERVINGS

1. Preheat oven to 325°F. Place a Dutch oven over medium heat. Cut the bacon into 1" pieces and add to the pot. Cook until they start to turn crispy and remove. Drain all but 1 tablespoon of the drippings.

2. Rinse the chicken under cold water and pat the pieces dry. Combine the flour, salt, and pepper in a wide, shallow bowl. Dredge the pieces through the flour and place them skin-side down in the skillet. Cook for 3–4 minutes on each side, or until they're lightly honey colored. Cook in batches if necessary.

3. Remove the chicken once it's cooked and add the broth, wine, mustard, and garlic. Turn off the heat and place the chicken back in the Dutch oven. Tuck the thyme and bay leaves amongst the chicken. Sprinkle the celery, carrots, and onion on top of the chicken. Cover and put in the oven. Cook for 2–2½ hours.

4. Remove the chicken and vegetables to a large bowl and cover to keep warm. Discard the thyme and bay leaves. Place the Dutch oven over medium-high heat and let most of the liquid evaporate. Stir in a tablespoon of flour and whisk quickly to keep from getting lumps. Once you have thick gravy, pour it over the chicken pieces in the bowl and serve warm.

4 SLICES BACON

1 FRYER CHICKEN OR 3-4 POUNDS OF CHICKEN THIGHS

½ CUP FLOUR

1 TEASPOON SALT

¼ TEASPOON GROUND PEPPER

1 CUP CHICKEN BROTH

2 CUPS DRY RED WINE

2 TABLESPOONS DIJON MUSTARD

2 GARLIC CLOVES, MINCED

3-4 STALKS FRESH THYME

3 BAY LEAVES

2 CELERY STALKS

2 CARROTS

1 MEDIUM ONION

2-3 TABLESPOONS FLOUR

Senegalese Chicken

YIELDS 6–8 SERVINGS

1. Mix everything but the chicken, 2 tablespoons of oil, cabbage, and carrots in a gallon-sized sealable plastic bag. Add the chicken and toss to combine. Marinate for 4–24 hours.

2. Place a large skillet over medium-high heat. Once it's heated, add 2 tablespoons of peanut oil. Place a few pieces of chicken in the skillet and cook for 4–5 minutes on each side until just browned. Remove the chicken to a dish. You may have to sauté the chicken in batches.

3. Once the chicken is sautéed, remove the onions from the marinade and cook for 10–12 minutes. Add the rest of the marinade and the vegetables to the skillet. Cover and boil for 10 minutes, or until the carrots are not quite tender.

4. Place the chicken back in the pot, cover with a lid, and cook for 20 minutes. Stir occasionally. Serve over rice or couscous.

½ CUP PEANUT OIL

4 MEDIUM ONIONS, ROUGHLY SLICED

2 LEMONS, JUICED

4 LIMES, JUICED

½ CUP APPLE CIDER VINEGAR

2 BAY LEAVES

4 GARLIC CLOVES, CHOPPED

2 TABLESPOONS PREPARED MUSTARD

1 SERRANO PEPPER, CLEANED AND DICED

1 TEASPOON SALT

½ TEASPOON BLACK PEPPER

1 5-6 POUND STEWING CHICKEN, CUT INTO INDIVIDUAL PIECES

2 TABLESPOONS PEANUT OIL

½ CABBAGE, CUT INTO CHUNKS

3 CARROTS, PEELED AND CHUNKED

Chicken Breast Rotolo with Currant Stuffing

YIELDS 1 SERVING

1. Use the flat end of a meat tenderizer or a rolling pin to pound the chicken breast until it's ⅜" thick. Sprinkle each side with salt and pepper.

2. Place a small skillet over medium heat. Place pine nuts in the skillet and shake every 30 seconds to 1 minute and turn off the heat as soon as you smell them toasting. Transfer nuts to a separate container.

3. Place the small skillet back over medium heat. Once it is warm, add 1 tablespoon olive oil, vegetables, and garlic. Stir the vegetables frequently for 5–7 minutes. Add the currants and cook for 1 minute until warm. Use the back of a spoon to crush them. Cook for 3–4 minutes. Once most of the juices have evaporated, stir in herbs and nuts.

4. Spoon the mixture onto the widest end of the chicken breast and roll toward the narrow end. Use kitchen twine or toothpicks to hold it together. Wipe out the skillet.

5. Place the skillet over medium heat. Once heated, add 1 tablespoon olive oil. Place the chicken in the skillet and cook for 2–3 minutes, make a quarter turn, and cook for another 2–3 minutes. Continue cooking and turning for 8–12 minutes. Remove twine or toothpicks and slice the chicken into ¾" rounds. Serve immediately.

1 CHICKEN BREAST HALF

PINCH SALT

PINCH PEPPER

2 TABLESPOONS PINE NUTS OR OTHER NUT

2 TABLESPOONS OLIVE OIL

½ CELERY STALK, MINCED

¼ SMALL YELLOW ONION, MINCED

1 SMALL GARLIC CLOVE, MINCED

¼ CUP FRESH CURRANTS

1 TABLESPOON FRESH THYME OR BASIL, CHOPPED

2 TABLESPOONS FRESH PARSLEY, CHOPPED

Rapini and Black Olive–Stuffed Chicken Breast

YIELDS 1 SERVING

1. Preheat oven to 350°F. Place the chicken breast on a sturdy surface. Use the flat side of a meat tenderizer to pound the breast until it is about ⅜" thick. Sprinkle both sides with salt and pepper.

2. Place a skillet over medium-high heat. Once heated, add 1 tablespoon olive oil, the rapini, and the onion. Cook for several minutes until the leaves are wilted and the stems are softened.

3. In a bowl, combine the rapini and onion, garlic, olives, and Parmesan cheese. Place the mixture near the widest end of the chicken breast and roll toward the other end. Use cooking twine or toothpicks to keep in place.

4. Place the small skillet back over medium-high heat. Once warmed, add 1 teaspoon oil to the pan and add the chicken. Brown for 1 minute on each side. Transfer the skillet to the middle of the oven and cook for 35–40 minutes.

5. Remove the twine or toothpicks and cut the roll in slices. Serve immediately.

1 CHICKEN BREAST

PINCH SALT

PINCH BLACK PEPPER

1 TABLESPOON PLUS 1 TEASPOON OLIVE OIL

2 OUNCES RAPINI, CHOPPED

¼ SMALL ONION, CHOPPED

1 GARLIC CLOVE, MINCED

2 OUNCES PITTED BLACK OLIVES, MINCED

1 TABLESPOON SHREDDED PARMESAN CHEESE

Chapter 8

SEAFOOD ENTRÉES

Pan-Seared Scallops and Chorizo

1. If using a firm sausage in casing, slice into ¼" rounds.

2. Place a skillet over medium heat. Once heated, add the chorizo. If cooking rounds of sausage, cook 3 minutes or until lightly crispy on each side. If using loose sausage, spread the sausage evenly over the bottom of the skillet and cook for 5–7 minutes, or until the sausage is cooked through. Break up the sausage into bite-sized chunks.

3. Remove the chorizo and place in a bowl. Drain off all but 1 tablespoon of oil from the skillet. Add the scallops to the skillet and cook for 1 minute on each side.

4. Return the chorizo to the skillet, pour the lemon juice over, and sprinkle with ground pepper while stirring to coat.

5. Remove the chorizo and scallops to plates and sprinkle fresh parsley on top.

6 OUNCES CHORIZO SAUSAGE

1 POUND SCALLOPS, CUT IN HALF IF LARGE

JUICE FROM 1 LEMON

FRESH GROUND PEPPER TO TASTE

¼ CUP CHOPPED FRESH PARSLEY

Smothered Whitefish with Caramelized Onions

YIELDS 4 SERVINGS

1. Preheat oven to 350°F. Sprinkle the fillets with salt and pepper on each side. Place a skillet over medium heat to preheat. Once it is heated, add the oil and the fillets.

2. Turn off the heat and cover each fillet with ¼ cup caramelized onion. Place the skillet in the oven and cook for 20 minutes. The fish is cooked through when it starts to flake apart. Serve hot.

4 6-OUNCE WHITEFISH FILLETS

SALT TO TASTE

PEPPER TO TASTE

1 TABLESPOON OLIVE OIL

1 CUP CARAMELIZED ONIONS

Curried Crabmeat

YIELDS 4 SERVINGS

1. Place a skillet over medium heat. Once it is heated, add the butter. Once the butter stops foaming, add the onion, stirring frequently for 3 minutes, or until the onion is softened.

2. Stir the flour into the skillet with the curry powder to create a paste. Stir the paste continually for 2 minutes.

3. Slowly pour in the chicken broth, whisking continually to prevent lumps. Bring to a simmer and cook for 3 minutes.

4. Stir in the crabmeat and cook until heated. Remove from the heat and serve over rice.

2 TABLESPOONS BUTTER

¼ SMALL ONION, CHOPPED

3 TABLESPOONS FLOUR

2 TEASPOONS CURRY POWDER

2 CUPS CHICKEN BROTH

1½ CUPS CRABMEAT

Halibut Creole

1. Preheat oven to 400°F. Place a large skillet over medium heat. Add the butter, lemon juice, and Tabasco sauce. Stir until the butter has melted. Turn off the heat.

2. Season the fish on each side with salt and pepper. Sprinkle the onion and bell pepper over the bottom of the skillet. Add the fish to the skillet and pour the tomatoes over the fish.

3. Bake for 20–25 minutes, or until the thickest part of the fish is opaque. Spoon the pan juices over the fish every 10 minutes. Remove it from the pan and spoon the sauce over the fish to serve.

4 TABLESPOONS BUTTER

JUICE FROM 2 LEMONS

SEVERAL DASHES TABASCO SAUCE

4 8-OUNCE HALIBUT STEAKS

PINCH SALT

PINCH PEPPER

1 SMALL ONION, CHOPPED

½ RED BELL PEPPER, CHOPPED

3 LARGE TOMATOES, PEELED, SEEDED, AND CHOPPED

Tamarind Tuna

1. Place the tamarind pulp in a glass bowl. Heat the water and pour it over the paste. Use a spoon to combine the pulp with the water.

2. Sprinkle the tuna lightly with the salt. Cut it into 1½" strips. Add the tuna to the marinade and toss to coat. Let it sit for 30 minutes at room temperature.

3. Place a skillet over medium-high heat. When it is warmed, add the oil. Pat the tuna dry and add to the oil when it's hot. Cook for 2 minutes on each side. The tuna will be dark on each side but still pink in the center. Serve over white rice.

½ CUP TAMARIND PULP

1 CUP WATER

1 POUND TUNA FILLET

½ TEASPOON SALT

¼ CUP PEANUT OIL

Cajun Shrimp with Beer Sauce

YIELDS 4 SERVINGS

1. Rinse the shrimp and shake them dry. Combine all of the dried seasonings in a bowl.

2. Place a skillet over medium-high heat. When it is hot, add the butter and garlic and cook for 1 minute. Add the seasoning mix, Worcestershire sauce, and beer.

3. Once the sauce bubbles, add the shrimp. Cook for 4–6 minutes, stirring so they cook evenly.

4. Once the shrimp are cooked, remove from the pan and place in a serving bowl. Let the liquid simmer for 10 minutes until it is a reduced sauce. Adjust the seasonings and serve with white rice.

1 POUND SHRIMP, PEELED AND DEVEINED

¼ TEASPOON CAYENNE PEPPER

1 TEASPOON BLACK PEPPER

1 TEASPOON SALT

1 TEASPOON RED CHILI FLAKES

1 TEASPOON THYME

1 TEASPOON OREGANO

1 TEASPOON GROUND MARJORAM

4 TABLESPOONS UNSALTED BUTTER

3 CLOVES GARLIC, MINCED

2 TEASPOONS WORCESTERSHIRE SAUCE

1 CUP BEER, ROOM TEMPERATURE

Fish Tacos with Serrano Pepper White Sauce

YIELDS 2 SERVINGS

1. *For White Sauce:* Peel, seed, and mince the serrano pepper. Mix with yogurt, mayonnaise, and garlic salt. Refrigerate for 3 hours.

2. *For Fish Tacos:* Rinse fish and pat dry with paper towels. Place a skillet over medium-high heat. Once it is heated, add the oil and swirl to coat. Add the fillets, skin-side up. Shake the skillet to prevent sticking. Cook for 3 minutes.

3. Flip the fish over and cook for another 3 minutes. You should see the side of the fish change from translucent to opaque. Remove the fish from the pan and place it skin-side up on a plate. Carefully peel off the skin.

4. Chop the fish into 1" strips and place in a bowl. Sprinkle salt and squeeze the lime over the top of the fish. Toss to coat. Serve in tortillas with toppings and sauce.

WHITE SAUCE

1 SERRANO PEPPER

¼ CUP YOGURT

¼ CUP MAYONNAISE

1 TEASPOON GARLIC SALT

FISH TACOS

½ POUND FIRM WHITEFISH FILLETS

2 TABLESPOONS PEANUT OR CORN OIL

SALT TO TASTE

1 LIME

4 CORN TORTILLAS

SHREDDED CABBAGE TO TASTE

DICED TOMATO TO TASTE (OPTIONAL)

WHITE SAUCE TO TASTE

FISH TACOS WITH SERRANO
PEPPER WHITE SAUCE

Seared Tuna Steak with Tangy Cilantro Sauce

YIELDS 2 SERVINGS

1. Roughly chop the cilantro. Place in a blender with the water, 2 teaspoons salt, and vinegar. Pulse on liquefy for several minutes until the contents are smooth. Pour the safflower oil in slowly while the blender runs. Taste and season with salt as needed.

2. Rinse the tuna under cold water and pat dry. Sprinkle with salt and pepper. Place a skillet over medium-high heat. Once it is heated through, add the garlic cloves and olive oil. Toss to coat and move the cloves to the edges of the pan.

3. Place the tuna in the middle of the skillet and cook for 2 minutes on the first side. Flip it to the second side and cook for 1 minute. This will make it rare.

4. If you prefer a medium-done tuna, cook for 4 minutes on the first side and 3 minutes on the second with the skillet over medium heat.

5. Slice the steak against the grain and drizzle the cilantro sauce over the fish. Serve while warm.

1 BUNCH CILANTRO, RINSED AND PICKED OVER

¼ CUP WATER

2 TEASPOONS PLUS 1 PINCH SALT

¼ CUP RICE WINE VINEGAR

½ CUP SAFFLOWER OR CANOLA OIL

1 12–16-OUNCE TUNA STEAK

PINCH PEPPER

2 GARLIC CLOVES, PEELED AND SMASHED

1 TABLESPOON OLIVE OIL

SEARED TUNA STEAK WITH TANGY CILANTRO SAUCE

Tuna Almandine with Sugar Snap Peas

YIELDS 2 SERVINGS

1. Place a large skillet over medium-high heat. Add the butter and sliced onions. Stir frequently for 8–10 minutes or until they're tender and translucent.

2. Add the peas to the skillet and season with salt and pepper. Toss them a few times and cook for 2–3 minutes. Move the vegetables to the sides of the skillet. If the butter in the skillet has evaporated, add some olive oil.

3. Place the tuna steaks in the middle of the skillet and cook on each side for 2–3 minutes. You'll want the center to be pink, so cooking to medium-rare is recommended. Divide the tuna and peas between two plates and sprinkle the almonds on top.

2 TABLESPOONS BUTTER

½ LARGE SWEET ONION, THINLY SLICED

½ POUND SUGAR SNAP PEAPODS

SALT TO TASTE

PEPPER TO TASTE

1 TABLESPOON OLIVE OIL

2 6-OUNCE TUNA STEAKS

½ CUP SLICED ALMONDS

Shrimp and Avocado Pasta with a Tequila Tomato Sauce

YIELDS 8 SERVINGS

1. Put half the avocado, tomatoes, salt, pepper, and red pepper flakes in a blender and pulse several times. You don't want a thin purée but do want to chop up the tomatoes and avocado and mix with the spices.

2. Place a skillet over medium-heat and add half of the butter. Cut the other half into cubes and set aside. Once the butter has melted, add the shrimp and tequila to the skillet. Stir quickly to combine and stir every 2 minutes until the shrimp are slightly pink and the tequila has mostly evaporated. Reduce the heat to low.

3. Cook fettuccine according to package directions. Add the contents of the blender and the remaining butter to the skillet. Stir to combine. Add the remaining avocado and cilantro as garnish on the final dish. Once the pasta is cooked through, drain and divide into bowls. Pour the sauce and shrimp over each dish and garnish with avocado and cilantro.

1 AVOCADO, PEELED AND CHOPPED

1 28-OUNCE CAN CHOPPED TOMATOES

1 TEASPOON SALT

¼ TEASPOON FRESHLY GROUND BLACK PEPPER

1 TEASPOON CRUSHED RED PEPPER FLAKES

3 TABLESPOONS COLD UNSALTED BUTTER

1½ POUNDS MEDIUM SHRIMP

½ CUP TEQUILA

1 POUND FETTUCCINE

¼ CUP FRESH CILANTRO, CHOPPED

Shrimp in Fra Diavolo Sauce

YIELDS 4–6 SERVINGS

1. Cook the linguini according to the package directions. Place a skillet over medium heat. Once it is heated, add 1 tablespoon of olive oil, shrimp, red pepper flakes, and salt. Stir frequently for 2 minutes to keep everything from sticking.

2. Turn off the heat and pour in the sweet wine. Toss and let sit for 2 minutes. The residual heat should cause most of the wine to evaporate. Pour the contents into a bowl and set aside.

3. Return the skillet to the stove over low heat. Once it is heated, add 2 tablespoons of olive oil and the garlic. Cook for several minutes. Once it starts to turn golden brown, remove from the oil and set aside to drain. If the oil gets frothy, lower the heat.

4. Stir in more red pepper flakes if desired, tomatoes, and the dry wine. Increase the heat to medium and simmer for 10 minutes to reduce. Stir in parsley. Divide pasta and top with the shrimp and sauce.

1 POUND LINGUINI

3 TABLESPOONS OLIVE OIL

1 POUND DEVEINED AND SHELLED SHRIMP (31–40 COUNT)

1 TEASPOON RED PEPPER FLAKES

1 TEASPOON SALT

¼ CUP SWEET WHITE WINE

4 CLOVES GARLIC, THINLY SLICED

1 15-OUNCE CAN CHOPPED TOMATOES

1 CUP DRY WHITE WINE

¼ CUP PARSLEY, CHOPPED

French or Belgian Steamed Mussels

YIELDS 2 SERVINGS

1. Fill a very large bowl half full of water that is cool to the touch. Sprinkle the cornmeal across the top of the water and let it settle. Use a plastic bristle brush to remove any dirt or other unwanted debris from the mussels. To remove the beard, place the back of a butter knife on one side of the beard and your thumb on the other side. Pinch the beard between your thumb and the knife and pull using a side-to-side motion.

2. Place mussels into the bowl. Shake the bowl every few minutes to keep the cornmeal floating. Let them sit in the water for 30 minutes. Every 10 minutes gently nudge the bowl to create waves. The mussels should expel any dirt they have stored and replace it with the cornmeal.

3. Place a Dutch oven over medium heat and add the butter. Add the onions and stir to coat in butter. Stir frequently until they are mostly translucent. Add the garlic and stir. Cook for 3–4 minutes. Add the wine and herbs. Cover and bring to a boil.

4. Remove the lid and gently add mussels to the pan, leaving the dirt in the bottom of the bowl. When all of the mussels are added, increase the heat to high and cook for 3–4 minutes.

5. Scoop the mussels into bowls and keep them warm. Discard any that haven't opened. Let the liquid in the pan continue to boil for 5–10 minutes until reduced by half. Pour the liquid and onions over the mussels. Serve with crusty bread.

WATER, AS NEEDED

1 CUP CORNMEAL

2 POUNDS FRESH MUSSELS

2 TABLESPOONS BUTTER

1 MEDIUM YELLOW ONION, THINLY SLICED

1 LARGE GARLIC CLOVE, MINCED

2 CUPS DRY WHITE WINE OR ALE

3 TABLESPOONS FRESH TARRAGON OR THYME, CHOPPED

Oysters Rockefeller

1. Preheat oven to 450°F. Combine the white part of the scallion, celery, parsley, and spinach. Chop them together till very fine. Place into a bowl with the bread crumbs, Tabasco, and Worcestershire sauce.

2. Cream the butter and salt into the bread crumb mixture until you get a fine paste. Pour 1" of rock salt over the bottom of the skillet. Nestle the oysters in the salt.

3. Divide the butter and bread crumb mixture over the oysters. Bake for 10 minutes, or until the mixture has melted. Sprinkle a pinch of green scallion on top of each oyster and serve while warm with lemon wedges.

1 SCALLION, CHOPPED, WHITE AND GREEN PARTS SEPARATED

¼ CELERY STALK, FINELY CHOPPED

2 TABLESPOONS FRESH PARSLEY, CHOPPED

¼ CUP FRESH SPINACH, CHOPPED

2 TABLESPOONS UNSEASONED BREAD CRUMBS

3 DASHES TABASCO

¼ TEASPOON WORCESTERSHIRE SAUCE

2 TABLESPOONS BUTTER

½ TEASPOON SALT

ROCK SALT, AS DESIRED

12 LARGE OYSTERS ON THE HALF-SHELL

1 LEMON, CUT INTO 8 WEDGES

Scallops Seared in Clarified Butter

YIELDS 4 SERVINGS

1. Use several paper towels to pat the scallops dry. Wrap them in paper towels and let them sit at room temperature for 15 minutes. If there is a tough muscle on the side, remove it.

2. Place a skillet over medium-high heat. Once it is warmed, add the clarified butter. Season the scallops with salt and pepper and place in the pan.

3. Cook for 2–3 minutes, or until the bottom edges start to turn golden brown. Flip them over and cook for 2–3 minutes, or until the sides are opaque.

4. Remove the scallops from the pan. Add the butter, garlic, thyme, and wine. Scrape the bottom to remove the crust. Let the wine boil for 5 minutes. Pour it over the scallops and serve with lemon wedges and fresh parsley, if desired.

12 WHOLE SCALLOPS

3 TABLESPOONS CLARIFIED BUTTER (CHAPTER 6)

PINCH SALT

PINCH PEPPER

2 TABLESPOONS BUTTER

2 GARLIC CLOVES

1 TEASPOON DRIED THYME

1 CUP DRY WHITE WINE

1 LEMON, CUT INTO WEDGES

CHOPPED FRESH PARSLEY TO TASTE (OPTIONAL)

Seafood Paella

1. Bring 2 quarts of water to a boil. Stir in ¼ cup salt and sugar until dissolved. Add several cups of ice cubes till chilled. Add the shrimp to the brine, cover, and refrigerate overnight. Remove from the brine and pat dry. Sprinkle with 1 tablespoon of oil, 2 garlic cloves, 1 pinch salt, and pepper. Let it sit at room temperature for 30 minutes.

2. Preheat oven to 350°F with a rack just below the middle position.

3. Place a very large skillet or a Dutch oven over medium heat. Add 1 tablespoon of oil and the bell pepper. Cook for 5–7 minutes. Spoon the pepper out and set aside, but leave as much of the oil in the pan as possible.

4. Add 2 tablespoons of oil to the pan, add the onion, and cook for 5–7 minutes. Add the remaining garlic, stirring continually for 1 minute. Stir in 1 cup of water, the tomatoes, chicken broth, rice, wine, bay leaves, saffron, and 1 pinch salt. Increase the heat to medium-high and bring to a boil.

5. When the contents boil, cover and cook in the middle of the oven for 15–20 minutes. Gently stir the seafood into the rice. Lay the pepper strips in a pinwheel on top and sprinkle the peas across the top. Cook in the oven for 8–12 minutes.

6. Rest for 5 minutes before serving. Discard any unopened mussels and the bay leaves. Serve with parsley and lemon wedges.

2 QUARTS PLUS 1 CUP WATER

¼ CUP PLUS 2 PINCHES SALT

¼ CUP SUGAR

ICE CUBES, AS NEEDED

1 POUND LARGE SHRIMP, PEELED AND DEVEINED

4 TABLESPOONS OLIVE OIL

6 GARLIC CLOVES, MINCED

PINCH PEPPER

1 RED BELL PEPPER, SEEDED AND SLICED

1 MEDIUM WHITE ONION, FINELY CHOPPED

1 15-OUNCE CAN DICED TOMATOES

1 15-OUNCE CAN CHICKEN BROTH

2 CUPS WHITE RICE

½ CUP DRY WHITE WINE

3 BAY LEAVES

1 LARGE PINCH SAFFRON THREADS

12 MUSSELS, CLEANED AND DEBEARDED

1 CUP CLEANED SQUID, SLICED IN RINGS

2 CUPS CRABMEAT

1 CUP FROZEN PEAS, THAWED

¼ CUP CHOPPED PARSLEY

1 LEMON, CUT IN WEDGES

Tamarind Shrimp Kebabs

YIELDS 4 SERVINGS

1. Combine the tamarind paste and broth in a bowl. Let it sit for several minutes and then mash the paste until it has dissolved. Add the wine, sugar, and salt, stirring to combine.

2. Trim wooden skewers to fit your pan. Combine the garlic, onion, and jalapeño, and rub on the cut side of the shrimp. Thread the shrimp onto skewers so they're barely touching. Place the skewers in a large dish and lay flat. Pour the marinade over the shrimp, cover, and place in the refrigerator for 30–60 minutes.

3. Place a grill pan over medium-high heat and brush the ridges with the peanut oil. Remove the skewers from the marinade and place one layer on the pan. Cook for 3–4 minutes on each side. Once they're pink on both sides, place on a serving platter.

4. Sprinkle the scallion and cilantro over the platter for serving. If you want to serve the leftover marinade as a dipping sauce, pour the liquid into a small skillet and bring to a boil and cook for 2–3 minutes. Serve alongside the shrimp.

2 TABLESPOONS TAMARIND PASTE

½ CUP CHICKEN OR VEGETABLE BROTH

2 TABLESPOONS RICE WINE OR DRY SHERRY

1½ TABLESPOONS BROWN SUGAR

½ TEASPOON SALT

4 GARLIC CLOVES, MINCED

1 SMALL YELLOW ONION, MINCED

1 JALAPEÑO, MINCED

1 POUND SHELL-ON SHRIMP (31–40 COUNT), DEVEINED

1 TEASPOON PEANUT OIL

2 SCALLIONS, CHOPPED

¼ CUP CILANTRO, CHOPPED

Grilled and Butter-Basted Lobster Tails

1. Place the lobster tail on the cutting board shell-side down. Cut through the belly shell from the top, through the meat, and through the back shell. Don't cut through the fin portion of the tail. Gently pull the sections of meat away from the shell. Rinse the tails in cold water.

2. Combine the chives and 1 tablespoon of olive oil in a small bowl. Rub the mixture over the meat and shell.

3. Place a grill pan over high heat. Once it's heated through, brush the surface of the pan with the remaining olive oil. Place the lobster shell-side down on the grill. Cover and cook for 1 minute. Turn the lobster and cook on the other side for 1 minute, covered. The lobster should still be pink in the middle. Remove it from the pan.

4. Lower the heat to medium and add the butter. Once the butter has melted, add the garlic and water and rotate back and forth to combine. Bring to a simmer.

5. Hold the skillet at an angle so the sauce pools to one side. Place the lobster back in the pan on the side farthest away from the flame. Use a long-handled spoon to scoop butter and pour it over the lobster. Baste with the pan at an angle for 5 minutes, or until the lobster is cooked through. Sprinkle with parsley, pour the remaining sauce over the lobster, and serve.

2½ POUNDS LOBSTER TAILS

2 TABLESPOONS CHIVES, MINCED

2 TABLESPOONS OLIVE OIL

2 TABLESPOONS BUTTER

2 GARLIC CLOVES, MINCED

¼ CUP WATER

2 TABLESPOONS CHOPPED PARSLEY

Miso-Glazed Salmon

1. Combine the vinegar and mirin in a saucepan over medium heat until it is very warm but not boiling. Stir in the miso paste and dissolve. Cool to room temperature.

2. Rinse off the salmon fillets, remove any bones, and pat dry. Place them inside a sealable plastic bag. Pour the cooled mixture over the fillets and coat. Place in the refrigerator and let it sit for at least 8 hours, but no more than 3 days.

3. Place your grill pan over medium-high heat. Brush the ridges with vegetable oil. Once the pan is heated, place the salmon skin-side up. Cook for 3 minutes. Turn the fish to cook for 3 minutes on the other side. At this point the fish should be medium-rare. But if you prefer the fish cooked more thoroughly, turn the fish flesh-side down and place the fish at a different angle. Cook for 2 minutes on each side.

4. Place the leftover marinade in a saucepan over medium-high heat and bring to a boil. Boil for several minutes so it reduces to a syrup and brush or pour over the fish.

¼ CUP RICE WINE VINEGAR

¼ CUP MIRIN

¼ CUP RED MISO

4 6-OUNCE SALMON FILLETS

2 TABLESPOONS VEGETABLE OIL

Spanish Griddle-Cooked Shrimp

YIELDS 4 SERVINGS

1. Toss the tomatoes, green onion, cilantro, garlic, and salsa in a bowl and set aside. Toss the shrimp with the salt and pepper.

2. Place a griddle over medium-high heat. Once it's heated, pour 1 tablespoon of oil in the center of the pan and swirl to coat. Place half the shrimp on the pan so they aren't touching and cook for 1 minute. Remove the shrimp from the pan and place in a bowl. Repeat with 1 tablespoon of oil and the remaining shrimp.

3. Sprinkle the lime juice over the tomato mixture. Pour the mixture into the middle of the griddle and spread it out. Stir gently until the tomatoes are well heated. Sprinkle the partially cooked shrimp on top of the mixture. Cook for 2 minutes, or until they're cooked through and hot. Transfer to a large platter and serve with lime wedges.

3 MEDIUM TOMATOES, SEEDED AND CHOPPED

3 GREEN ONIONS, THINLY SLICED

¼ CUP CHOPPED CILANTRO LEAVES

3 GARLIC CLOVES, MINCED

¼ CUP SPICY TOMATO SALSA

1½ POUNDS LARGE SHRIMP, PEELED AND DEVEINED

DASH SALT

DASH PEPPER

2 TABLESPOONS OIL

JUICE FROM 1 LIME

1 LIME, CUT INTO WEDGES

Whole Salt-Crusted Red Snapper

YIELDS 4–6 SERVINGS

1. Preheat oven to 350°F. Place a rack in the middle of the oven. Rinse the fish under cold water and pat dry.

2. Mix the thyme, lemon, parsley, bay leaves, and onion together in a large bowl. Stuff most of the mixture into the cavity of the fish. Put a few slices of onion on the griddle. Place the fish on top of the onions.

3. Place the egg whites in a bowl and use a hand mixer to whip them to a stiff peak. Fold the salt into the egg whites to create a paste and smear over the fish. Place the griddle in the oven and cook for 35 minutes.

4. Crack the egg white shell and remove the large chunks. If the skin doesn't come off with the crust, peel it away. Use a long, skinny spatula to lift the top fillet off the skeleton. Carefully pull the skeleton off the fish and discard it. Separate the second fillet from the skin. Serve immediately.

1 WHOLE 3-4-POUND RED SNAPPER, CLEANED AND GUTTED WITH SCALES, GILLS, AND FINS REMOVED

¼ CUP THYME

1 LEMON, SLICED

¼ CUP PARSLEY, CHOPPED

2 BAY LEAVES

1 SMALL YELLOW ONION, THINLY SLICED

4 EGG WHITES

1 CUP COARSE OR KOSHER SALT

Deep-Fried Tuna with Spicy Garlic Sauce

YIELDS 2 SERVINGS

1. Combine the soy sauce, garlic, ginger, pepper, sake, fish sauce, and chili sauce in a small bowl. Refrigerate overnight.

2. Just before cooking the tuna, stir cornstarch into the cold sauce. Warm the sauce in a microwave or a small saucepan, stirring frequently to thicken. Sprinkle the tuna with salt and pepper lightly.

3. Place a fryer over medium heat. Once the oil is heated, add two pieces of tuna and cook for 1 minute. Remove them from the oil and pat dry with paper towels. Repeat with the remaining tuna. Slice the tuna into ½" slices and pour the sauce over them. Serve while hot.

2 TABLESPOONS SOY SAUCE

2 GARLIC CLOVES, MINCED

½ TEASPOON FRESH GINGER, GRATED

½ TEASPOON GROUND BLACK PEPPER

¼ CUP SAKE

1 TABLESPOON FISH SAUCE

½ TEASPOON CHILI SAUCE

1 TABLESPOON CORNSTARCH

4 4-OUNCE TUNA FILLETS

PINCH SALT

PINCH PEPPER

1 QUART VEGETABLE OIL

Cornmeal-Battered Catfish

YIELDS 4–6 SERVINGS

1. Rinse the fillets and cut them into 2"-thick slices. Combine the cornmeal, flour, salt, pepper, and cayenne in a wide, shallow bowl. In a separate wide, shallow bowl whisk together the eggs and the beer.

2. Dredge the catfish in the flour, then the beer mixture, and then in the flour again. Place on a wire rack and rest for 10 minutes.

3. Place a fryer over medium heat and add the oil. Once the oil is heated, carefully slide 3–4 pieces of fish into the oil. Cook until lightly browned. Flip halfway through. Remove them from the oil and dry on a wire rack with paper towels underneath. They will darken as they cool. Serve with tartar sauce, remoulade, or garlicky mayo.

2 POUNDS CATFISH FILLETS

½ CUP YELLOW CORNMEAL

¼ CUP ALL-PURPOSE FLOUR

1½ TEASPOONS SALT

¼ TEASPOON GROUND BLACK PEPPER

PINCH CAYENNE

2 EGGS, BEATEN

1 12-OUNCE BEER, LAGER-STYLE

3 CUPS VEGETABLE OIL

Salmon with Pineapple Salsa and Polenta

YIELDS 1 SERVING

1. *For Pineapple Salsa:* Finely chop pineapple rings and place in a small skillet with minced red onion, minced red pepper, juice from one lime, and chopped cilantro. Place over medium heat, salt lightly, and stir frequently for 15 minutes. The juices should evaporate and the onion and pepper should soften.

2. *For Salmon:* Preheat broiler to high. Sprinkle the salmon lightly on each side with salt. Place a small skillet over medium-high heat. Once hot, add the oil and place the fillet in the middle of the pan. Cook for 3 minutes on the first side and 2 minutes on the second side. Brush 1 tablespoon of the salsa on top. Place it in the oven about 4" from the flame for 30 seconds, just enough to caramelize the salsa. Place the fish on a plate and let it rest.

3. Place the skillet over medium-high heat. Slice 2½" thick slices from the tube of polenta. Once the skillet is hot, add the oil and slide the 2 patties into the skillet. Don't touch them for 4 minutes. There should be enough crust on the bottom of the polenta to keep it together. Use a spatula to flip the polenta and cook for 5 minutes on the second side.

4. Once the polenta is cooked, drain off excess oil. Place the salmon on top of the polenta, pour the remaining salsa on top of the salmon, and place the skillet back in the oven for 1 minute to warm the fish through. Serve it immediately with the lime wedge.

PINEAPPLE SALSA

5 PINEAPPLE RINGS

2 TABLESPOONS MINCED RED ONION

2 TEASPOONS MINCED RED PEPPER

JUICE FROM 1 LIME

2 TEASPOONS CHOPPED CILANTRO

PINCH SALT

SALMON

1 6-OUNCE SALMON FILLET

PINCH SALT

1 TEASPOON PLUS 2 TABLESPOONS OLIVE OIL

3 TABLESPOONS PINEAPPLE SALSA

1 REFRIGERATED TUBE OF PRE-MADE POLENTA

1 LIME WEDGE FOR GARNISH

Sautéed Shrimp and Mushrooms

YIELDS 1 SERVING

1. Place a small skillet over medium heat. Once it is heated, add the butter and olive oil. Add the mushrooms, green onion, and a dash of salt. Cook for 4–5 minutes.

2. Stir in the tomato and garlic and cook for 3–4 minutes, or until the garlic smells fragrant and the tomato is starting to break down. Stir in the lemon juice. Cook for 1 minute.

3. Stir in the wine, the shrimp, and the Old Bay. Cook for 3–5 minutes, or until the shrimp turns pink. Serve while warm.

1 TABLESPOON BUTTER

1 TABLESPOON OLIVE OIL

¼ CUP SLICED MUSHROOMS

1 GREEN ONION, THINLY SLICED

DASH SALT

1 SMALL TOMATO, CORED AND DICED

1 GARLIC CLOVE, MINCED

JUICE FROM 1 LEMON

2 TABLESPOONS DRY WHITE WINE OR VERMOUTH

¼ POUND MEDIUM SHRIMP, SHELLED AND DEVEINED

¼ TEASPOON OLD BAY SEASONING

Chapter 9

PORK ENTRÉES

Kielbasa with Worcestershire Sauce, Potatoes, and Peppers

YIELDS 4 SERVINGS

1. Place a skillet over medium heat. Once it is heated, add the oil and the potatoes. Cook for 3 minutes. Stir and cover with a lid. Cook for another 5 minutes, stirring occasionally.

2. Add the onions and the peppers. Cook for 3 minutes, covered. Add the kielbasa and chicken broth. Cook for 8–10 minutes, or until the kielbasa is cooked through and the potatoes are browned. Stir in the Worcestershire sauce and season with salt and pepper to taste.

3 TABLESPOONS VEGETABLE OIL

4 MEDIUM POTATOES, CUT INTO ¼" SLICES

1 SMALL ONION, CHOPPED

1 BELL PEPPER, SEEDED AND CUBED

1 POUND KIELBASA, CUT INTO 1" PIECES

½ CUP CHICKEN BROTH

1 TABLESPOON WORCESTERSHIRE SAUCE

2 TEASPOONS SALT

¼ TEASPOON GROUND BLACK PEPPER

Oven-Roasted Skillet Spareribs

YIELDS 4 SERVINGS

1. Preheat oven to 350°F. Season the spareribs generously with salt and pepper on all sides.

2. Place the ribs in a large skillet in the middle of the oven. Bake for 30 minutes.

3. Turn them over and bake for another 30 minutes. If the ribs aren't crispy on the outside, increase the heat to 425°F and bake for 10 minutes. Serve while warm.

4 POUNDS SPARERIBS

SALT TO TASTE

PEPPER TO TASTE

Sweet-and-Sour Pork

YIELDS 4 SERVINGS

1. Place a skillet over medium heat. Combine the ketchup, lemon juice, and soy sauce. Add the sauce to the skillet.

2. Stir in the juice from the can of pineapple. Combine the cornstarch and water in a small bowl. Once the sauce is bubbling, whisk in the cornstarch mixture.

3. Let the sauce simmer for several minutes until it starts to thicken. Stir in the pork cubes and pineapple chunks. Cook until the sauce has thickened again and the pork is warmed through. Serve over white rice.

¼ CUP KETCHUP

JUICE FROM 1 LEMON

2 TEASPOONS SOY SAUCE

1 15-OUNCE CAN PINEAPPLE CHUNKS IN JUICE

1 TABLESPOON CORNSTARCH

¼ CUP COLD WATER

1 POUND COOKED PORK, CUBED

Southern-Style Pork Chops

YIELDS 6 SERVINGS

1. Rinse the pork chops and pat dry. Combine all of the dried spices together in a wide, shallow bowl. Place the flour in another wide, shallow bowl.

2. Rub the seasoning mix into each piece. Dredge the pork chops in the flour and shake off the excess. Place chops on a wire rack for 30 minutes before cooking.

3. Add the vegetable oil to a skillet and place over medium heat. When the oil is shimmering and hot, slide 2 pork chops into the skillet and cook on each side for 10–12 minutes. Place the cooked pork chops on paper towels and keep warm. Repeat with the other pork chops. Serve while warm.

6 PORK CHOPS, CUT 1" THICK

2 TEASPOONS SALT

2 TEASPOONS GARLIC POWDER

1½ TEASPOONS GROUND MUSTARD

1 TEASPOON SMOKED PAPRIKA

½ TEASPOON BLACK PEPPER

¼ TEASPOON ONION POWDER

½ TEASPOON DRIED OREGANO

½ CUP FLOUR

½ CUP VEGETABLE OIL

Italian Sausage with Escarole and White Beans

YIELDS 4–6 SERVINGS

1. Remove the thick stems and any thick veins from the escarole. Rinse the leaves in cold water to remove any dirt. Shake to dry or pat dry between a few towels.

2. Slice the sausage into ¼" slices. Place a skillet over medium-high heat and add the oil and sausage once the skillet is heated. Sprinkle garlic over the sausage. Toss to combine. Add the can of beans, including the juice, and chili flakes. Cook until the liquid has mostly evaporated.

3. Reduce the temperature to low and add the greens. Cover the pan with a lid and steam for 5–7 minutes to wilt and warm the greens. Dish onto plates and sprinkle with 1–2 teaspoons of the cheese.

1 BUNCH ESCAROLE

1½ POUNDS ITALIAN SAUSAGE LINKS, MILD OR HOT

3 TABLESPOONS OLIVE OIL

3 GARLIC CLOVES, MINCED

1 CAN CANNELLINI BEANS

½ TEASPOON RED CHILI FLAKES

¼ CUP ROMANO CHEESE, GRATED

Choucroute

1. Place a skillet over medium heat. Once it is heated, add the bacon to the skillet and fry until cooked through but not crispy. Add the onion and cook for 5–7 minutes, or until the onion starts to brown. Add the garlic and cook for 1 minute, stirring continually.

2. Add the apples, sauerkraut, and beer. Stir to combine. Add the juniper berries, peppercorns, bay leaves, and the sugar. Reduce the heat to low, cover, and simmer for 1 hour.

3. Stir the ham into the skillet and add the sausages. Cook for 1½ hours, covered. Add water to the pan if it seems like it is getting too dry. When the sausages are cooked through, serve while warm with boiled and buttered potatoes.

4 SLICES BACON

1 LARGE YELLOW ONION, CHOPPED

3 GARLIC CLOVES, SLICED

2 APPLES, CORED AND SLICED

1 QUART SAUERKRAUT, FRESH, JARRED, OR BAGGED

1 BOTTLE NON-BITTER BEER OR ½ BOTTLE RIESLING

7 JUNIPER BERRIES OR ½ CUP GIN

8 PEPPERCORNS

2 BAY LEAVES

1 TABLESPOON BROWN SUGAR

¼ POUND HAM, CUBED

1½ POUNDS GERMAN SAUSAGES (KNACKWURST, BRATWURST, GARLIC SAUSAGE, KIELBASA)

Icelandic Sweet and Tangy Pork

1. Cut the pork tenderloin into 2" chunks. Mix all the spices together in a bowl. Rub the spices over the pork. Let sit in the refrigerator for 2–24 hours.

2. Place a large skillet over medium-high heat. Once it is heated, add the oil and the pork. Don't crowd the pan, so do this in batches if necessary. Cook for about 2 minutes on each side. When all of the pork is browned, return all the pork to the skillet, lower the heat to medium-low, and add the beef broth.

3. Add the dates to the skillet and cook for 15–20 minutes. The pork should be barely pink in the middle.

4. While the pork cooks, place a small saucepan over medium heat and add the cream. Once it's heated, stir in the mustard until dissolved. Once dissolved, pour into the skillet. Place the cover on the skillet and cook for another 10 minutes. The pork should be completely cooked through and still tender.

3 POUNDS PORK TENDERLOIN

1 TEASPOON PAPRIKA

½ TEASPOON SALT

½ TEASPOON SUGAR

LARGE PINCH MUSTARD POWDER

½ TEASPOON CHILI POWDER

½ TEASPOON GROUND CUMIN

LARGE PINCH BLACK PEPPER

½ TEASPOON GARLIC POWDER

LARGE PINCH CAYENNE PEPPER

1 TABLESPOON VEGETABLE OIL

1 14-OUNCE CAN BEEF BROTH

1 POUND PITTED DATES, CHOPPED

1 PINT HEAVY CREAM

3 TABLESPOONS STONE-GROUND MUSTARD

JAMAICAN PORK AND MANGO STIR-FRY

Jamaican Pork and Mango Stir-Fry

YIELDS 4 SERVINGS

1. *For Jamaican Spice Mix:* Add all ingredients to a small bowl and stir to combine. Store the mixture in an airtight container. The flavors will start to diminish after 3 months but should be usable for up to a year.

2. *For Stir-Fry:* Trim any excess fat from the meat and slice into 1" rounds. Cut slices into ¼" strips. Sprinkle the spice mix over the pork and let it rest in the refrigerator for 4–8 hours, or on the counter for 30 minutes.

3. Place a skillet over medium heat. Once it is heated, add the oil and pork. Toss continually for 2 minutes. Add the ginger, mango, and bell pepper and cook for another 2–4 minutes, or until the pork is no longer pink.

4. Whisk the orange juice, cornstarch, and the Scotch bonnet pepper in a small bowl. Pour into the skillet, stirring continually. Cook for 2–3 minutes till the sauce has thickened.

5. Sprinkle the green onion over the dish and serve it over rice while warm.

JAMAICAN SPICE MIX

2 TABLESPOONS BROWN SUGAR

1 TABLESPOON KOSHER SALT

1 TABLESPOON CORIANDER

1 TABLESPOON GINGER

1 TABLESPOON GARLIC POWDER

½ TABLESPOON GROUND BLACK PEPPER

½ TABLESPOON CAYENNE PEPPER

½ TABLESPOON GROUND NUTMEG

½ TABLESPOON GROUND CINNAMON

STIR-FRY

1 POUND PORK TENDERLOIN

1 TEASPOON JAMAICAN SPICE MIX

2 TEASPOONS OLIVE OIL

1" CUBE FRESH GINGER, FRESHLY GROUND

1 MANGO, PEELED AND CUBED

1 RED BELL PEPPER

⅔ CUP ORANGE OR APPLE JUICE

1 TEASPOON CORNSTARCH

1 SCOTCH BONNET PEPPER, MINCED

¼ CUP SLICED GREEN ONION

Apricot-Stuffed Pork Roast

YIELDS 6 SERVINGS

1. Preheat oven to 425°F. Trim away most of the fat from the roast, but leave a thin layer on top. Cut ten evenly spaced holes that are 1½" deep. Rub a pinch of oregano into each hole. Add a piece of ginger, a piece of garlic, and a piece of apricot into each hole. Combine the rest of the oregano with the caraway seeds, the salt, and the pepper. Rub the roast with 1 tablespoon of oil, and rub the herb and spice mixture over the roast.

2. Place a skillet over medium-high heat. Once the skillet is heated, add the roast, fat-side down, and cook on each side for 5 minutes.

3. Once all of the sides are browned, remove the skillet from the heat and place it in the middle of the oven. Roast for 40–60 minutes or until the center of the roast registers 150°F. Remove the roast from the pan, cover with foil, and let it rest for 10 minutes while you make the sauce.

4. Place the chicken stock, 1 tablespoon of oil, shallots, and the balsamic vinegar in the skillet and place over medium heat. Use a spoon to scrape up any stuck-on bits. Cook for 8 minutes, or until slightly reduced. Whisk in the butter and season to taste with salt and pepper. Remove from the heat and serve in a bowl to pour over the roast.

1 3-POUND PORK ROAST

2 TEASPOONS FINELY CHOPPED FRESH OREGANO (OR 2 TABLESPOONS DRIED)

3" PIECE FRESH GINGER, PEELED AND CUT INTO 10 SLICES

5 GARLIC CLOVES, CUT INTO HALVES

5 APRICOTS, CUT INTO HALVES

1 TABLESPOON CARAWAY SEEDS

1 TEASPOON SALT

¼ TEASPOON GROUND BLACK PEPPER

2 TABLESPOONS OLIVE OIL

2 CUPS CHICKEN STOCK

2 SHALLOTS, MINCED

½ CUP BALSAMIC VINEGAR

1 TABLESPOON BUTTER

Pork Chop Cacciatore with Juniper Berries and Dried Rosemary

YIELDS 4 SERVINGS

1. Preheat oven to 450°F. Combine the olive oil, garlic, rosemary, and juniper in a bowl. Rub half the mixture on the pork chops and sprinkle with salt and pepper. Toss the potatoes and peppers in the bowl to coat with oil and spices. Sprinkle with salt and pepper.

2. Place a large skillet over medium-high heat. Once it is heated through, add the pork chops and cook on each side for 2–3 minutes. Remove from the heat.

3. Add the potatoes and peppers to the skillet, placing the chops on top of the vegetables. Bake for 15–20 minutes, or until the chops are just cooked through.

4. If the chops cook before the vegetables are done, remove the meat from the pan and set aside to keep warm. Change the oven to broil and cook for a few minutes while stirring frequently to prevent it from burning.

½ CUP OLIVE OIL

6 GARLIC CLOVES, MINCED

1 TABLESPOON DRIED ROSEMARY, CRUSHED

6 JUNIPER BERRIES, CRUSHED

4 BONE-IN PORK CHOPS, ½"–¾" THICK

SALT TO TASTE

PEPPER TO TASTE

2 LARGE BAKING POTATOES, HALVED AND CUT INTO THICK SLICES

2 BELL PEPPERS, SEEDED AND CUT INTO LARGE PIECES

Pork Chops with Capers and Mustard Sauce

YIELDS 4 SERVINGS

1. Trim off any excess fat from the pork chops. Rinse and pat dry. Sprinkle each side lightly with salt and pepper.

2. Place a large skillet over medium-high heat. Once it is heated, add the oil and pork chops. Cook on each side for 5 minutes until evenly browned. Place them on a plate and cover with foil.

3. Pour the broth into the pan and use a spoon to remove any stuck-on bits. Boil. Whisk in the capers, mustard, and butter. Once the butter has melted, return the chops to the skillet and continue cooking for 3–5 minutes until no pink juices run from a small cut in the center. Place them on a plate and cover with the foil again.

4. Turn the heat up to high and reduce the liquid in the pan by half before pouring over the chops and serving.

4 9-OUNCE PORK CHOPS (1¼" THICK)

SALT TO TASTE

PEPPER TO TASTE

1 TABLESPOON OLIVE OIL

1 CUP LOW-SODIUM CHICKEN OR VEGETABLE BROTH

⅓ CUP CAPERS

2 TABLESPOONS DIJON MUSTARD

2 TABLESPOONS SWEET CREAM BUTTER

Pork-Stuffed Chili Relleno

YIELDS 6 SERVINGS

1. Preheat oven to 375°F. Place a skillet over medium heat. Once it has heated, add the pork. Cook for 2 minutes on each side until browned. Cook in batches if necessary. Once the pork is seared, add half the onion, 4 smashed garlic cloves, and 1 teaspoon salt.

2. Add water to the skillet until the meat is barely covered. Braise in the oven for 45 minutes until the meat is tender but not soft. Remove the skillet from the oven and cool at room temperature until the pork can be handled. Shred the meat and discard any large pieces of fat or cartilage. Strain the broth and set aside. Discard the garlic and onion.

3. Wipe the skillet clean and place over medium-high heat. Once it is heated, add the oil and the remaining onion. Cook for 4–5 minutes. Add 3 minced garlic cloves and cook for 1 minute, stirring continually.

4. Add the meat and sprinkle the pepper, cinnamon, and cumin on top. Stir to combine and cook for 10 minutes. Add the tomato purée and cook for 10 minutes, or until the sauce has mostly evaporated. The mixture should be moist but not juicy.

5. Preheat the broiler. Cut the top off the poblano peppers and remove the seeds. Stuff about ½ cup of pork mixture into each pepper.

6. Lay the stuffed peppers in a clean skillet and place the skillet 6" from the flame. Roast evenly on each side for 3–4 minutes, or until the skins of the peppers just start to blacken and crack. Serve.

2 POUNDS PORK, CUT INTO 1" CUBES
1 WHITE ONION, CHOPPED
7 GARLIC CLOVES
1 TEASPOON SALT
WATER, AS NEEDED
3 TABLESPOONS VEGETABLE OIL
½ TEASPOON GROUND BLACK PEPPER
1 TEASPOON GROUND CINNAMON
1 TEASPOON GROUND CUMIN
1 15-OUNCE CAN TOMATO PURÉE
6 POBLANO CHILIES

PORK SCALLOPINE WITH RED WINE AND MUSHROOMS

Pork Scallopine with Red Wine and Mushrooms

YIELDS 4 SERVINGS

1. Use a meat tenderizer to pound the pork till it is ¼" thick. Season with salt and pepper. Dredge the pieces in flour and shake off the excess.

2. Place a large skillet over medium-high heat. When it's heated, add 2 tablespoons butter. Once it is melted and frothy, slide the pork into the skillet and cook for 1–2 minutes on each side. Remove them from the pan and set aside to stay warm.

3. Add the rest of the butter and the shallots to the skillet. Cook for 1 minute. Add the garlic to the pan and cook for 30 seconds.

4. Sprinkle the mushrooms, green beans, red bell pepper, thyme, and salt over the pan's surface. Cook for 5 minutes, stirring frequently until the mushrooms are tender.

5. Add the wine to the skillet and simmer for 10 minutes or until reduced by half. Taste and season as needed. Serve over rice or mashed potatoes.

1½ POUNDS PORK TENDERLOIN, CUT INTO 4 SLICES

SALT TO TASTE

PEPPER TO TASTE

½ CUP ALL-PURPOSE FLOUR

4 TABLESPOONS BUTTER

2 LARGE SHALLOTS, CHOPPED

2 GARLIC CLOVES, MINCED

16 OUNCES BUTTON MUSHROOMS, SLICED

½ CUP GREEN BEANS, CHOPPED

½ CUP RED BELL PEPPER, CHOPPED

1 TABLESPOON DRIED THYME

2 CUPS DRY RED WINE

Stuffed Pork Chops

1. Rinse the pork chops. Pat dry.

2. Place a skillet over medium heat. Once it's heated, add 1 tablespoon of the oil and the onion. Cook for 5–7 minutes. Add the mushrooms and cook for 7–10 minutes, or until they've softened and released their juices. Stir in the garlic clove and cook for 1 minute. Stir in the bread crumbs, parsley flakes, sugar, oregano, cheese, 1 teaspoon salt, and ¼ teaspoon pepper.

3. Preheat oven to 400°F.

4. Cut a pocket in each pork chop. Season the pork chops inside and out with salt and pepper. Divide the stuffing into 4 portions and stuff 1 portion into each chop.

5. Place a skillet over medium-high heat. Once heated, add the remaining oil and as many pork chops as will fit without touching. Cook on each side for 3–4 minutes until they're golden brown.

6. Place all the chops in the skillet and cook in the oven for 10 minutes until they're cooked through. Remove and let rest for 5 minutes before serving.

4 THICK-CUT BONELESS PORK CHOPS

2 TABLESPOONS OLIVE OIL

1 SMALL YELLOW ONION, CHOPPED

4 OUNCES BUTTON MUSHROOMS, CHOPPED

1 GARLIC CLOVE, MINCED

5 SLICES STALE BREAD, AIR-DRIED AND CRUMBED

1 TABLESPOON PARSLEY FLAKES

1 TEASPOON SUGAR

1 TEASPOON DRIED OREGANO

2 TABLESPOONS PARMESAN CHEESE

1 TEASPOON SALT PLUS MORE TO TASTE

¼ TEASPOON PEPPER PLUS MORE TO TASTE

Bacon-Wrapped Pork Tenderloin

YIELDS 4 SERVINGS

1. Cut the tenderloin into 1½" slices.

2. Place a skillet over medium-low heat. Once it is heated, add one bacon slice per pork medallion to the skillet. Cook slowly for about 8–10 minutes. When it starts to brown (not crisp), place on paper towels to drain. Discard all but 2 tablespoons of the bacon fat from skillet.

3. Season the medallions with pepper. Wrap one piece of bacon around each medallion and use a toothpick to keep in place, or tie with kitchen twine.

4. Place the skillet over medium-high heat. Once it is heated, place 3–4 medallions in the skillet so they're not touching. Cook for 5 minutes on each side. Then balance the medallions on their sides and cook in 1-minute increments, slowly rolling the medallions until the bacon is crispy on all sides and the center of the pork registers at 145°F. Transfer to a plate to keep them warm.

5. Add the remaining ingredients to the skillet, stirring until the browned bits are scraped off the bottom of the skillet. Let it simmer for 35 minutes. The contents should be thickened. Place the pork in the skillet and cook for 1 minute on each side to reheat. Serve with the sauce poured over the pork.

1½ POUNDS PORK TENDERLOIN, TRIMMED

8–10 SLICES BACON, 1 PER PORK SLICE

PEPPER TO TASTE

¼ CUP MAPLE SYRUP

2 GARLIC CLOVES

1 TABLESPOON BALSAMIC VINEGAR

2 TABLESPOONS DIJON MUSTARD

PINCH SALT

Seared and Roasted Pork Belly

YIELDS 4 SERVINGS

1. Rinse the pork belly and remove any loose pieces along the edges. Place the salt, sugar, and 4 cups of water into a small saucepan over medium heat. Stir frequently until the salt and sugar are dissolved. Place the pork belly into a sealable container that is deeper than the pork belly, but not much wider. Stir ice into the pan of water. Once the ice is melted, pour the mixture over the pork. Refrigerate for 12–24 hours.

2. Preheat oven to 300°F. Remove the pork from the brine and rinse it. Pat it dry and cut it into four even pieces. Place them in the bottom of a small Dutch oven. Pour in ½ cup of water and the broth. Sprinkle the garlic cloves and peppercorns around the pan. Cover with a lid, place in the middle of the oven, and cook for 2½ hours. The pork should be very tender.

3. Drain the liquid and peppercorns from the pan. Save the garlic cloves. Turn the pork over so it is fat-side down. Smear a garlic clove over the meaty side of each slice of pork. Place the Dutch oven over high heat and cook for about 3–5 minutes, or until the fat is crispy and golden brown. Serve immediately.

1¼ POUNDS BONELESS, SKINLESS PORK BELLY

¼ CUP SALT

½ CUP SUGAR

4½ CUPS WATER

2 CUPS ICE

½ CUP CHICKEN BROTH

5 GARLIC CLOVES

10 PEPPERCORNS

Japanese Pork Cutlets

YIELDS 4 SERVINGS

1. Whisk the soy sauce, mustard, honey, ketchup, and Worcestershire sauce together. Set aside.

2. Preheat oven to 200°F and place a baking pan in the middle of the oven.

3. Place the cornstarch in a wide, shallow bowl. Place the eggs in a second wide, shallow bowl and beat 1 tablespoon of vegetable oil into eggs. Place the panko in a third wide, shallow bowl.

4. Pat the pork dry with paper towels. Season with salt and pepper. Dip pork lightly in the cornstarch and shake to remove any excess. Dip pork in the egg and let the excess drain off. Lay the cutlet in the panko and make sure the meat is covered. Place on a wire rack and let dry for 5 minutes. Repeat with the other cutlets.

5. Once the pork breading has dried, place ½ cup of oil in a skillet over medium-high heat. The oil is hot enough for frying when a piece of breading dropped in the oil sizzles and floats. Place two cutlets in the oil and cook them until the bottom side is golden brown, about 2–3 minutes. Turn them over and let them cook for another 2 minutes. Place them on the baking pan in the oven to stay warm. Drain the oil, wipe the skillet, and repeat with the remaining oil and pork.

6. Serve whole or sliced with the sauce.

2 TEASPOONS SOY SAUCE

1 TEASPOON YELLOW MUSTARD

1 TEASPOON HONEY

½ CUP KETCHUP

2 TEASPOONS WORCESTERSHIRE SAUCE

½ CUP CORNSTARCH

2 LARGE EGGS

1 CUP VEGETABLE OIL

3 CUPS PANKO-STYLE BREAD CRUMBS

4 BONELESS PORK LOIN CHOPS, ¼" THICK

SALT TO TASTE

PEPPER TO TASTE

Pork Tenderloin Medallions Marinated in Currants

YIELDS 4 SERVINGS

1. Remove any external fat and silver-skin from the tenderloin. Cut into eight even slices. Sprinkle with salt and pepper on both sides.

2. Combine the vinegar, garlic, currants, and hot sauce in a sealable bag. Remove the air from the bag and use a rolling pin to break up the fruit. Add the pork to the bag and marinate from 30 minutes to 24 hours.

3. Place a grill pan over medium-high heat. When it's heated, add the oil. Cook the pork for 2 minutes on each side.

4. Remove the pork from the pan and keep warm. Pour the marinade into a skillet. Bring to a boil, reduce the heat to low, and add the pork. Cook on each side for another 2 minutes.

5. Remove the pork from the pan, pour the sauce over the pork, and serve while warm with cilantro or parsley.

1 2-POUND PORK TENDERLOIN

PINCH SALT

PINCH PEPPER

3 TABLESPOONS BALSAMIC VINEGAR

1 GARLIC CLOVE, MINCED

½ CUP FRESH RED CURRANTS

½ TEASPOON HOT SAUCE

1 TABLESPOON OLIVE OIL

¼ CUP FRESH CILANTRO OR PARSLEY, CHOPPED

Italian Sausages and Sweet Peppers

YIELDS 2 SERVINGS

1. Place a grill pan over medium heat and when it's heated place the sausages at one end. Place the vegetables, oil, basil, and oregano in a bowl and toss to combine. Spread the vegetables over the rest of the grill pan.

2. Cook the sausages for 4 minutes on each side. Toss the vegetables every few minutes. Reduce the heat to low, cover the pan, and steam the sausages in the liquid created by the vegetables. Stir the vegetables every few minutes. Cook each side for another 8 minutes.

3. Remove the sausages and vegetables from the skillet and keep warm. Increase the heat to medium-high. Pour the chicken stock in the pan so it coats the surface. Scrape any stuck-on bits. Simmer for 4 minutes. Pour the liquid over the vegetables and sausages and serve.

2 SWEET ITALIAN SAUSAGE LINKS

1 SMALL ONION, THICKLY SLICED

½ RED BELL PEPPER, SLICED

½ GREEN BELL PEPPER, SLICED

1 TABLESPOON OLIVE OIL

1 TEASPOON DRIED BASIL

1 TEASPOON DRIED OREGANO

¼ CUP CHICKEN STOCK

Brown Sugar Teriyaki Pork

YIELDS 3–4 SERVINGS

1. Place the garlic and ginger in a small saucepan over medium heat with the soy sauce, 1 cup water, and brown sugar. Bring to a boil.

2. Dissolve the cornstarch in ¼ cup cold water and stir until there are no lumps. Slowly add the cornstarch mixture to the saucepan, whisking continuously. Bring back to a boil and thicken slightly. Remove from the heat and cool to room temperature.

3. Slice the pork loin into ½" slices. Pound them lightly with a meat tenderizer. Place in a bowl and add the marinade. Refrigerate for 30 minutes.

4. Preheat broiler. Place a griddle pan over medium-low heat. Lay the pork slices on the pan and cook on each side for 2 minutes. Use a brush to baste each side of the pork.

5. Place the pan 4" from the broiler and cook each side for 2 minutes. The center of the meat should no longer be pink. The sugars in the marinade will become shiny and caramelized.

1 GARLIC CLOVE, MINCED

1 TABLESPOON FRESHLY GRATED GINGER

¼ CUP SOY SAUCE

1 CUP PLUS ¼ CUP COLD WATER

3 TABLESPOONS BROWN SUGAR

2 TABLESPOONS CORNSTARCH

1 POUND PORK LOIN

Dutch Oven Cassoulet

YIELDS 6–8 SERVINGS

1. Sort the cannellini beans and remove any debris. Cover with water by several inches in a large bowl and soak overnight.

2. Place a large Dutch oven over medium-high heat. Place the duck legs skin-side down in the pan and cook each side for 3–4 minutes. Remove and add the sausage, browning each side. Remove and add the lamb. Cook for 8–10 minutes until browned on each side. Remove and add the bacon. Cook until it starts to render its fat. Add the ham hocks and cook until browned on all sides. Remove the hocks.

3. Add the onion, carrot, and celery to the bacon. Cook for 10 minutes, or until the vegetables have softened and the bacon is crispy. Add 5 minced garlic cloves and cook for 1 minute.

4. Add the broth, tomato paste, bay leaves, and thyme. Stir till blended. Increase heat and bring to a boil. Add the beans and meat. Cover and reduce the heat to low. Simmer for 3–4 hours. Turn off the heat.

5. Remove the meat from the pan. Cut the sausage into chunks and set aside. Remove the ham and duck meat from the bones and set aside. Skim the fat from the stew and add the paprika. Taste and add salt as necessary. Return the meat to the pan.

6. Turn on the broiler and set an oven rack on almost the lowest setting. Combine the bread crumbs, parsley, and remaining garlic and spread over the pan. Drizzle butter on top. Place the pan under the broiler and cook until browned. Serve warm.

1 POUND CANNELLINI BEANS

WATER, AS NEEDED

4 DUCK LEGS

1 POUND GARLICKY, NON-SPICY SAUSAGE

1 POUND LAMB SHOULDER, CUBED

½ POUND BACON, CUT INTO STRIPS

2 HAM HOCKS

1 LARGE ONION, ROUGHLY CHOPPED

2 LARGE CARROTS, ROUGHLY CHOPPED

2 CELERY STALKS, ROUGHLY CHOPPED

7 GARLIC CLOVES, MINCED

2 QUARTS CHICKEN BROTH

2 TABLESPOONS TOMATO PASTE

2 BAY LEAVES

2 TABLESPOONS FRESH THYME OR 2 TEASPOONS DRIED

1 TABLESPOON SWEET OR SMOKED PAPRIKA

SALT TO TASTE

2 CUPS BREAD CRUMBS

6 TABLESPOONS CHOPPED PARSLEY

2 TABLESPOONS MELTED BUTTER

Oven-Braised Pork Roast

1. Place a Dutch oven over medium-high heat. Place the fat side of the roast down in the pan. Cook for 4 minutes on each of its four sides. Remove it to a plate and let sit.

2. Place the onions and celery in the pan and cook for a few minutes before adding the broth. Stir to remove the fond from the bottom of the pan.

3. Add the garlic, peppercorns, salt, and allspice and stir to combine. Stir in the ale. Reduce the heat to low. Return the roast to the center of the pan. Cover and simmer for 3–3½ hours. The roast should be tender and easy to cut.

4. Remove the roast to a pan to keep warm. Use a stick blender to purée the vegetables left in the pan. Serve with mashed potatoes.

1 4-POUND PORK ROAST

1 LARGE ONION, CUT INTO THICK RINGS

2 CELERY STALKS, CUT INTO 1" PIECES

1 14-OUNCE CAN CHICKEN OR VEGETABLE BROTH

2 GARLIC CLOVES, SMASHED

7 WHOLE PEPPERCORNS

2 TABLESPOONS SALT

1 WHOLE ALLSPICE

1 12-OUNCE BOTTLE DARK ALE

Spaghetti Carbonara

YIELDS 2 SERVINGS

1. Place a pot of water over high heat, cover it, and let it come to a boil. Cook the pasta according to package directions.

2. Place a skillet over medium-low heat. Chop the meat into matchstick-sized pieces and add to the skillet when it is warm. Cook until crispy. Drain off all but 1 tablespoon of the drippings.

3. In a small bowl, whisk the eggs, cheese, pepper, and nutmeg. Increase the heat on the skillet to medium and add the wine. Stir occasionally and let the wine reduce until it is a light syrup. Add the butter and stir it until it melts. Reduce heat to low and let the skillet sit until the pasta is cooked.

4. Drain the spaghetti and pour it into the skillet. Toss to coat the spaghetti evenly with the sauce. Pour the egg mixture over the pasta and stir vigorously until the noodles are coated and the egg has set. Serve immediately.

4 OUNCES DRIED SPAGHETTI

3 TABLESPOONS PROSCIUTTO, PANCETTA, OR BACON

2 EGGS

¼ CUP PARMESAN CHEESE, GRATED

¼ TEASPOON GROUND BLACK PEPPER

PINCH NUTMEG

1 CUP WHITE WINE OR VERMOUTH

2 TABLESPOONS BUTTER

Croque Madame

1. Butter one side of each slice of bread. Spread the other side of each bread slice with a thin smear of mustard. Assemble two sandwiches using half of the cheese and ham on each. Make sure the buttered sides are on the outside of the sandwich.

2. Place a skillet over medium heat. When heated, place the sandwiches in the skillet. Cook each side for 3–4 minutes, or until they're toasted and golden brown. Remove to a plate and keep warm.

3. Place the remainder of the butter in the skillet. Once it has stopped foaming, slowly pour two eggs into the skillet. Sprinkle each egg with salt and pepper. Cover and let the eggs cook for 3–5 minutes, depending on how firm you like the yolks.

4. Center an egg on top of each sandwich, or inside for easier eating, and serve while warm.

2 TABLESPOONS BUTTER, SOFTENED

4 SLICES SOURDOUGH OR WHEAT BREAD

2 TEASPOONS DIJON MUSTARD

4 OUNCES GRUYÈRE OR EMMENTALER CHEESE, THINLY SLICED

5 OUNCES SLICED SMOKED HAM

2 EGGS

PINCH SALT

PINCH PEPPER

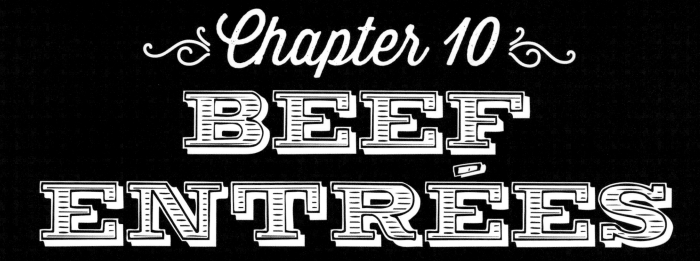

Chapter 10
BEEF ENTRÉES

Grilled Tenderloin with Chili and Cashews

YIELDS 4 SERVINGS

1. Cook the noodles according to package directions. Drain.

2. Rub 2 tablespoons of the chili sauce over the meat and season with salt and pepper. Place a grill pan over medium-high heat. Once it's heated, grill the steaks for 3–4 minutes on each side. Let rest for 5 minutes.

3. Combine 1 tablespoon of the chili sauce with the sesame oil, lime juice, and scallions. Toss the mixture over the noodles. Divide the noodles into 4 bowls.

4. Slice the beef thinly and place it over the noodles. Sprinkle the cashews over the beef and serve.

1 POUND THAI RICE NOODLES

3 TABLESPOONS ASIAN CHILI SAUCE

4 6-OUNCE FILET MIGNON PORTIONS

SALT TO TASTE

PEPPER TO TASTE

1 TABLESPOON TOASTED SESAME OIL

JUICE FROM 2 LIMES

3 SCALLIONS, THINLY SLICED

5 OUNCES CASHEWS, CRUSHED

Swiss Steak with Smoked Paprika

1. Preheat oven to 325°F. Trim any exterior fat from the steak. Mix the flour, salt, and pepper in a small bowl. Sprinkle half of the flour mixture over the roast and use the base of a sturdy glass to pound the flour into the meat. Repeat with the other side.

2. Place a skillet over medium heat. Once the skillet is heated, add the oil and the meat. Cook on each side for 5 minutes until the meat is browned.

3. Remove the meat from skillet and add the onion. Cook for 5 minutes, stir in the garlic. Chop the tomatoes and add. Stir in the paprika, Worcestershire, and broth. Add the meat to the skillet and cook covered in the oven for 2 hours, or until the meat is tender.

1½ POUNDS RUMP, ROUND, OR CHUCK ROAST

2 TABLESPOONS FLOUR

1 TEASPOON SALT

½ TEASPOON GROUND BLACK PEPPER

2 TABLESPOONS VEGETABLE OIL

1 MEDIUM ONION, THINLY SLICED

2 GARLIC CLOVES, SMASHED

1 15-OUNCE CAN STEWED TOMATOES

1 TEASPOON SMOKED PAPRIKA

1 TABLESPOON WORCESTERSHIRE SAUCE

1 CUP BEEF BROTH

Thai Mussamun Curried Beef

1. Place a skillet over medium heat. Once it's heated, add the oil and onion. Stir frequently and cook for 7–9 minutes, or until the onion is lightly browned. Stir in the dried spices, the ginger, and the chili and cook for 3–5 minutes, or until the spices are fragrant.

2. Remove the outer leaves from the lemongrass stalk. Cut off the base end and the top dried portion. Cut the stalk in half lengthwise and then into 1" chunks. Stir the lemongrass and the coconut milk into the skillet.

3. Add the cubed beef, soy sauce, and sugar to the skillet. Stir to combine and cook for 7–10 minutes. Serve over jasmine rice.

2 TABLESPOONS PEANUT OIL

1 LARGE YELLOW ONION, SLICED

1 TEASPOON DRIED CHILI POWDER

1 TEASPOON GROUND CORIANDER

1 TEASPOON GROUND CUMIN

½ TEASPOON BLACK PEPPER

½ TEASPOON GROUND NUTMEG

1" PIECE GINGER, PEELED AND SHREDDED

1 SERRANO OR THAI CHILI, THINLY SLICED

1 LEMONGRASS STALK

1 15-OUNCE CAN COCONUT MILK

½ POUND BEEF SIRLOIN, CUT INTO CUBES

1 TEASPOON SOY SAUCE

2 TEASPOONS SUGAR

Carne Guisada

1. Place a Dutch oven over medium-high heat. Add the oil and beef when it is heated. Cook for 5 minutes so all sides are browned. Remove the beef and set aside.

2. Add the onion and peppers and cook for 5 minutes while stirring frequently. Add the garlic, celery, and mushrooms and cook for 5 minutes. Once the celery has softened, add the beer. Stir to loosen the fond.

3. Add the tomatoes, jalapeños, cumin, and beef broth. Return the meat to the pan and stir until everything is well combined. Turn the flame to the lowest setting and cover. Cook for 3–3½ hours. The meat should fall apart when you pick it up. Serve immediately.

2 TABLESPOONS VEGETABLE OIL

1½ POUNDS BEEF STEW MEAT, TRIMMED AND CUBED

1 LARGE ONION, CUT INTO EIGHTHS

1 RED BELL PEPPER, SEEDED AND SLICED

4 GARLIC CLOVES

1 CELERY STALK, CHOPPED

8 OUNCES BUTTON MUSHROOMS, SLICED

1 CUP BEER

1 14-OUNCE CAN STEWED TOMATOES

2 FRESH JALAPEÑO PEPPERS, STEMMED, SEEDED, AND DICED

1 TEASPOON GROUND CUMIN

2 CUPS BEEF BROTH

GRILLED FLANK STEAK WITH CHIMICHURRI SAUCE

Grilled Flank Steak with Chimichurri Sauce

YIELDS 4 SERVINGS

1. Place a grill pan over high heat. Season the steak with a pinch of salt and pepper on both sides. Brush vegetable oil across the surface of the pan once it is heated.

2. Place the steak in the pan and cook for 4 minutes. Turn it and cook for 4 minutes for medium-rare, 5 minutes for medium, and 6 minutes for medium-well. Place the steak on a cutting board, tent with foil, and let it rest for 5 minutes.

3. Place the parsley in a food processor or blender and pulse several times. Scrape down the sides and add the garlic, scallion, and vinegars. Pulse a few times. Add in 1 teaspoon salt, ¼ teaspoon pepper, and the rest of the spices and pulse until smooth. While the food processor runs, slowly add the olive oil to create an emulsion.

4. Cut the steak diagonally against the grain into ½"-thick slices. Serve with the sauce and, if desired, garnish with grilled cherry tomatoes.

1½ POUNDS FLANK STEAK, TRIMMED OF EXCESS FAT

1 PINCH PLUS 1 TEASPOON SALT

1 PINCH PLUS ¼ TEASPOON GROUND BLACK PEPPER

2 TEASPOONS VEGETABLE OIL

2 CUPS PACKED PARSLEY LEAVES

4 GARLIC CLOVES, QUARTERED

1 SCALLION, ROUGHLY CHOPPED

¼ CUP APPLE CIDER VINEGAR

¼ CUP RED WINE VINEGAR

½ TEASPOON GROUND PAPRIKA

1 LARGE PINCH RED CHILI FLAKES

¼ CUP OLIVE OIL

GRILLED CHERRY TOMATOES FOR GARNISH, IF DESIRED

Japanese Caramelized Ribeye Steaks

1. *For Sweet Chili Sauce:* In a blender, add garlic cloves, honey, lime juice, fish sauce, and Thai red chili peppers. Purée until thin and add more lime juice if you want a thinner texture.

2. *For Steaks:* Preheat oven to 450°F and place a rack in the center of the oven.

3. Whisk together the lime juice, soy sauce, garlic, wasabi powder, and chili sauce.

4. Place a skillet over medium-high heat. Once it is heated, add half of the oil and two of the steaks. Cook on each side for 2 minutes. Repeat with the other steaks.

5. Turn off the heat, place all of the steaks in the skillet, and pour the sauce on the steaks. Cook in the oven for 7–10 minutes; 7 minutes for medium-rare and 10 minutes for medium-well.

6. If the steaks don't sit flat in the skillet, flip them halfway through the cooking time. Serve with white rice.

SWEET CHILI SAUCE

4 MINCED GARLIC CLOVES

2 TABLESPOONS HONEY

JUICE FROM 4 LIMES PLUS MORE AS NEEDED

2 TABLESPOONS FISH SAUCE

1-2 THAI RED CHILI PEPPERS, STEMMED AND CHOPPED

STEAKS

JUICE FROM 4 LIMES

½ CUP SOY SAUCE

3 GARLIC CLOVES, MINCED

1 TEASPOON WASABI POWDER

1 CUP SWEET CHILI SAUCE

4 6-OUNCE RIBEYE STEAKS

2 TABLESPOONS OLIVE OIL

Skillet-Seared Skirt Steak

YIELDS 4 SERVINGS

1. Trim as much of the silverskin and fat from the steak as possible. Cut each steak with the grain into 2 even pieces that are 4"–5" long.

2. Sprinkle the meat with salt. If desired, toss the steak in a sauce or a marinade.

3. Place a skillet over high heat. Once the skillet is hot but not smoking, add 1 tablespoon of oil to the pan. Slide half of the meat into the skillet. Cook for 3–4 minutes, or until browned. Shake the skillet frequently to keep the meat from sticking.

4. Use tongs to flip the steak to the other side and cook for 3–4 minutes. The meat should be medium to medium-rare. Cooking past medium will make the steak very tough. Remove the meat from the skillet and tent with foil to keep warm. Repeat with remaining meat.

5. Let the second batch of meat rest for 5 minutes. Slice thin against the grain and serve with a sauce of your choice while warm.

1½ POUNDS SKIRT STEAK

PINCH SALT

2 TABLESPOONS VEGETABLE OIL

Swedish Meatballs with Lemon and Honey Sauce

YIELDS 4–6 SERVINGS

1. Sprinkle 1 teaspoon salt over the onion and set aside. Cut the bread into cubes and place in a large bowl. Add the egg and milk and mash into a paste. Add the beef, pork, the onion, nutmeg, allspice, and pepper. Mix together with your hands. Use a tablespoon to create evenly sized meatballs.

2. Place skillet over medium-high heat and add enough oil so it is ½" deep. Once the oil is heated, add a single layer of meatballs so they don't touch. Roll them frequently so they brown evenly for 8–10 minutes. Reduce the heat if the oil starts to smoke. Place the meatballs on paper towels to drain and keep warm.

3. Drain the oil from the pan, but leave the brown bits. Add the butter; when it has melted and is just starting to turn brown, sprinkle the flour over the surface and whisk for about 1 minute.

4. Stir in the broth, honey, and bay leaves, whisking and scraping the bottom of the skillet. Bring the mixture to a simmer and cook for 5 minutes.

5. Once the sauce has thickened, stir in the milk. Return the meatballs to the skillet and simmer for about 5 minutes so they're heated through. Discard the bay leaves, stir in the lemon juice, and taste before adding salt and pepper. Serve with boiled egg noodles.

1 TEASPOON PLUS 1 PINCH SALT

1 SMALL ONION, MINCED

2 SLICES WHITE SANDWICH BREAD, CRUST REMOVED

1 LARGE EGG, BEATEN LIGHTLY

3 TABLESPOONS MILK

8 OUNCES LEAN GROUND BEEF

8 OUNCES GROUND PORK

LARGE PINCH NUTMEG

LARGE PINCH ALLSPICE

LARGE PINCH PEPPER

1–2 CUPS VEGETABLE OIL

1 TABLESPOON BUTTER

1 TABLESPOON ALL-PURPOSE FLOUR

2 CUPS CHICKEN BROTH

2 TEASPOONS HONEY

2 BAY LEAVES

½ CUP MILK

JUICE FROM 1 LEMON

Pomegranate Beef Teriyaki

YIELDS 4 SERVINGS

1. Whisk together the garlic, ginger juice, soy sauce, vinegar, sesame oil, and pomegranate juice. Place it in a sealable glass bowl. Add the beef strips to the marinade and let it rest in the refrigerator for 4–24 hours. Stir once or twice.

2. Place a large skillet over medium-high heat. Add the peanut oil once the pan is heated. Add half of the beef strips, stirring frequently. Cook for 4–5 minutes, or until browned. Remove the beef from the skillet and repeat with the rest of the beef. Return the first batch of the beef to the skillet and cook until most of the liquid has evaporated.

3. Add the frozen broccoli to the skillet and toss to combine. Pour the marinade over the skillet contents and toss to combine for about 3 minutes or until the broccoli is cooked through. Serve over rice.

1 GARLIC CLOVE, MINCED

1 TEASPOON GINGER JUICE

3 TABLESPOONS SOY SAUCE

3 TABLESPOONS RICE WINE VINEGAR

1 TEASPOON TOASTED SESAME OIL

3 TABLESPOONS POMEGRANATE JUICE

1½ POUNDS SIRLOIN, CUT INTO ¼" STRIPS

2 TABLESPOONS PEANUT OIL

3 CUPS FROZEN BROCCOLI

Bi Bim Bap

YIELDS 4–6 SERVINGS

1. Place the bean sprouts, carrots, cucumber, and vinegar in a small glass bowl. Toss to combine, press the vegetables so they are submerged, and let sit in the refrigerator for 4–24 hours. Drain the vegetables before serving.

2. Toss the beef and soy sauce together in a bowl. Cover and let sit for 30 minutes at room temperature. Preheat oven to 200°F and insert 4–6 oven-safe bowls.

3. Place a skillet over medium-high heat. Once it is warmed, add 1 tablespoon of oil, the beef, and the mushrooms. Cook for 2 minutes. Add 1 tablespoon of the oil and the garlic. Cook for 30 seconds. Add the spinach, sprinkle with salt and pepper, and toss until the spinach is wilted. Place a serving of rice into each bowl. Divide the beef and vegetables over the rice and place the bowls back in the oven.

4. Wipe the skillet clean and add 2 tablespoons of oil to the skillet. Place it over medium-high heat. Crack 2 eggs into 2 coffee mugs. Once the skillet is heated, pour the eggs into the skillet at the same time. Do not to break the yolks. Sprinkle salt and pepper on top, cover the skillet with a lid and cook for 2–3 minutes. The whites should be set, but the yolks should be runny. Repeat with remaining eggs.

5. Remove the bowls and slide 1 egg onto each bowl. Drizzle the sesame oil over the eggs and add a portion of the pickled vegetables to the bowl. Serve while hot.

2 CUPS BEAN SPROUTS

1 MEDIUM CARROT, PEELED AND GRATED

1 MEDIUM CUCUMBER, PEELED, HALVED, AND SLICED IN HALF ROUNDS

1 CUP RICE VINEGAR

8 OUNCES SIRLOIN, CUT INTO ¼"-THICK SLICES

2 TABLESPOONS SOY SAUCE

¼ CUP VEGETABLE OIL

12 OUNCES SHIITAKE MUSHROOMS, MINCED

4 GARLIC CLOVES, MINCED

1 POUND SPINACH, CLEANED, STEMMED, AND CHOPPED

PINCH SALT

PINCH PEPPER

6 CUPS COOKED RICE, WARM

4–6 LARGE EGGS

1 TABLESPOON SESAME OIL

Braised Beef Shank with Potatoes, Carrots, and Cauliflower

YIELDS 3–4 SERVINGS

1. Bring the meat to room temperature. Place a large skillet over medium-high heat. Add the butter and oil. Once it is heated, sear the meat on each side for 4 minutes. Add the peppercorns to the skillet and cook for 2 minutes. Add the onion to the pan and place the meat on top of the onion.

2. Stir the tomato paste into the water. Add it to the skillet with the balsamic vinegar. Bring the broth to a boil and then reduce the heat to low. Once it reduces to a simmer, skim off the foam and discard. Add the thyme and bay leaves. Cover the pan and cook for 3½–4 hours. Remove the meat and keep warm.

3. Strain the stock and return it to the pan. Add the garlic, carrots, potatoes, and cauliflower to the pan. Place it over medium heat and cook for 30 minutes, uncovered. Continue to skim off any foam as it cooks. Add salt and pepper to taste.

4. Separate the beef into pieces and pour the sauce over the meat. Serve with vegetables on the side.

2 PIECES BEEF SHANK, 2" THICK

2 TABLESPOONS BUTTER

4 TABLESPOONS VEGETABLE OIL

1 TABLESPOON DRY PEPPERCORNS

1 LARGE ONION, CHOPPED

1 5-OUNCE CAN TOMATO PASTE

2 QUARTS WATER

1 CUP BALSAMIC VINEGAR

2 TABLESPOONS FRESH THYME

2 BAY LEAVES

4 GARLIC CLOVES, MINCED

4 CARROTS, PEELED AND CUT INTO CHUNKS

3 MEDIUM POTATOES, PEELED AND CHUNKED

½ HEAD CAULIFLOWER, CUT INTO CHUNKS

SALT TO TASTE

PEPPER TO TASTE

Pepper Steak with Chilies and Cayenne

1. Place peppers over direct flame or in a grill pan over medium-high heat and cook for 12–15 minutes, turning frequently, until the skins are charred. Place the peppers in a tightly sealed bag and let them steam and cool for 2–3 minutes.

2. Trim the bottoms and tops off the peppers. Cut them open down one side and remove the seeds and ribs. Scrape off the charred skin and rinse clean. Slice the peppers into ½"-wide strips.

3. Place a large skillet over medium-high heat. Add 1 tablespoon of oil. Sprinkle salt and pepper on the meat and add to the skillet. Cook for 3–4 minutes on each side. Once cooked, remove it from the pan and cover.

4. Add the remaining oil to the skillet with the onions. Cook for 5–7 minutes. Add the garlic and cook for 1 minute. Add the vinegar and soy sauce and stir to scrape up any stuck-on bits. Add 1 cup of chicken broth.

5. Stir the cornstarch into the remaining chicken broth until there are no lumps. Stir the broth briskly into the pan to prevent lumping. Stir in the tomato sauce and basil. Bring the contents to a simmer.

6. Add the pepper strips and cayenne powder. Taste the broth and season if needed. Simmer for 3 minutes. Return the beef and warm for 2 minutes. Serve over rice.

12 POBLANO OR ANAHEIM CHILIES

2 TABLESPOONS VEGETABLE OR OLIVE OIL

PINCH SALT

PINCH PEPPER

1¼ POUNDS TENDERLOIN

1 LARGE SWEET ONION, THINLY SLICED

5 GARLIC CLOVES, MINCED

3 TABLESPOONS RED WINE VINEGAR OR RICE WINE VINEGAR

1 TABLESPOON SOY SAUCE

1½ CUPS CHICKEN BROTH

3 TABLESPOONS CORNSTARCH

½ CUP TOMATO SAUCE

1 TEASPOON DRIED BASIL

PINCH CAYENNE POWDER

3 CUPS COOKED RICE

New York Strips with Mustard Herb Crust

YIELDS 4 SERVINGS

1. Preheat oven to 425°F. Trim any extra fat from the steak. Sprinkle each side liberally with salt and pepper.

2. Place a skillet over medium-high heat. Once it's heated, add the oil. Cook the steaks for 1 minute on each side. Remove the skillet from the heat.

3. Cover both sides of the steaks with the mustard. Combine the bread crumbs, parsley, garlic, and butter in a bowl.

4. Place the steaks in a skillet and divide the bread crumbs mix over the 4 steaks. Place the skillet in the oven and bake for 12–15 minutes. Let the meat rest for 10 minutes before serving.

4 6-8-OUNCE NEW YORK STRIP STEAKS

SALT TO TASTE

PEPPER TO TASTE

1 TABLESPOON OLIVE OIL

3 TABLESPOONS GRAINY MUSTARD

¾ CUP BREAD CRUMBS

½ CUP PARSLEY, CHOPPED

2 GARLIC CLOVES, MINCED

3 TABLESPOONS BUTTER

Skirt Steak with Chermoula

YIELDS 4 SERVINGS

1. Trim off any membrane or extra fat from the beef. Brush the meat with vegetable oil and sprinkle with salt and pepper. Let it sit at room temperature for 30–60 minutes.

2. To make the chermoula, combine the remaining ingredients in a small bowl.

3. Place a grill pan over medium-high heat. Once it's heated, cook the meat for 3–5 minutes on each side. Let rest for 10 minutes before serving.

4. Slice the steak in thin slices on an angle and place them over steamed white rice and top with the chermoula. Leftovers can be stored in the refrigerator for up to 1 week.

1½ POUNDS SKIRT STEAK

2 TABLESPOONS VEGETABLE OIL

PINCH SALT

PINCH PEPPER

1 SMALL ONION, DICED

2 GARLIC CLOVES, MINCED

1 CUP PARSLEY, CHOPPED

½ CUP CILANTRO, CHOPPED

1 TEASPOON GROUND CUMIN

JUICE FROM 3 LEMONS, ZEST FROM 1

¼ TEASPOON CAYENNE

¼ TEASPOON GROUND BLACK PEPPER

½ TEASPOON SMOKED PAPRIKA

Spicy Beef and Chicken Fajitas

YIELDS 6–8 SERVINGS

1. Combine the beer, ½ cup vegetable oil, lime juice, garlic, Worcestershire sauce, chili powder, pepper, and cumin and divide into 2 large sealable bowls.

2. Trim any excess fat off the steak and chicken. Use a meat tenderizer to pound the chicken to ⅜" thick. Sprinkle the meat lightly with salt and place the beef in one container and the chicken in the other. Refrigerate for 3–8 hours.

3. Place a grill pan over medium-high heat and brush the ridges with oil. Place the onions on the pan and cook until translucent. Move to a bowl and keep warm. Scatter the peppers across the grill pan and cook until soft. Place them in the bowl with the onions.

4. Apply another coating of oil on the grill pan ridges. Cook the flank steak for 4–5 minutes on each side. Let it rest on a plate. Slice the steak into strips.

5. Apply another coating of oil on the grill pan ridges. Cook the chicken breasts for 6–7 minutes on each side. Let them rest on a plate. Slice the chicken into strips. Serve meat and vegetables with warm tortillas, chopped cilantro, lime wedges, and hot sauce or salsa.

12 OUNCES BEER

½ CUP VEGETABLE OIL PLUS MORE AS NEEDED

JUICE FROM 2 LIMES

5 GARLIC CLOVES, SMASHED

2 TABLESPOONS WORCESTERSHIRE SAUCE

1 TABLESPOON CHILI POWDER

1 TEASPOON GROUND BLACK PEPPER

1 TEASPOON GROUND CUMIN

1 POUND SKIRT OR FLANK STEAK

1 POUND BONELESS, SKINLESS CHICKEN BREASTS

SALT TO TASTE

2 SMALL ONIONS, QUARTERED

1 GREEN PEPPER, CUT INTO ½" STRIPS

1 RED OR YELLOW PEPPER, CUT INTO ½" STRIPS

CORN OR FLOUR TORTILLAS FOR 6-8 PEOPLE

CHOPPED FRESH CILANTRO

LIME WEDGES

BOTTLED HOT SAUCE OR SALSA TO TASTE

Beef Short-Rib Cholent

YIELDS 6–8 SERVINGS

1. The night before cooking, trim the excess fat off the ribs and cut into sections of 3–4 ribs. Sprinkle with salt and refrigerate in a tightly sealed container. Sort the beans and chickpeas and place in a large bowl. Cover with water by 2"–3". The day you're serving, place a rack in the middle of the oven and preheat oven to 200°F. Pat the meat dry with paper towels.

2. Place a 6–7-quart Dutch oven over medium heat. Add the vegetable oil and a few of the ribs. Sear each side for 4 minutes. Once all the meat is browned, place on a platter and pour off the fat.

3. Add the wine and scrape the bottom of the pan. Add the onions and cook for 5–7 minutes. Add the garlic cloves, brown sugar, paprika, cayenne pepper, cumin seeds, and pepper. Stir and cook for 2–3 minutes.

4. Drain the beans and chickpeas and spread over the onions. Lay the meat on top of the beans. Layer the potatoes on top and sprinkle the carrots on the potatoes. Nestle the eggs in the carrots. Add 4 cups of water gently so the layers don't move. Cover and place over medium-high heat. Bring to a boil.

5. Cook in the middle of the oven for 8 hours. Uncover the pan and skim off as much fat as possible. Place the layers around the edges of a platter and place the ribs in the center. Peel the eggs and cut in half. Use the braising liquid as a gravy and serve immediately.

3 POUNDS BONE-IN BEEF SHORT RIBS

SALT TO TASTE

½ CUP DRIED KIDNEY BEANS

½ CUP DRIED CHICKPEAS

WATER, AS NEEDED

1 TABLESPOON VEGETABLE OIL

1 CUP DRY RED WINE

1 POUND ONIONS, COARSELY CHOPPED

1 GARLIC HEAD, PEELED

2 TABLESPOONS BROWN SUGAR

1 TABLESPOON SWEET PAPRIKA

¼ TEASPOON GROUND CAYENNE PEPPER

1 TEASPOON CUMIN SEEDS

½ TEASPOON GROUND BLACK PEPPER

1 POUND BAKING POTATOES, PEELED AND QUARTERED

2 LARGE CARROTS, PEELED AND CUT INTO CHUNKS

4 LARGE EGGS

Dijon Mustard Steak Strips

YIELDS 1 SERVING

1. Place a skillet over medium-high heat and add oil. When it is heated, add the onion. Stir frequently and cook for 2–3 minutes, or until the onion is translucent. Add the steak to the pan and cook for 1 minute on each side.

2. In a small bowl, combine the beef broth, sour cream, mustard, soy sauce, and garlic powder. Pour over the beef. Cover the pan, reduce heat to low, and cook for 3–4 minutes for a medium-done steak.

3. Remove the lid, increase the heat to medium-high, and boil for 1–2 minutes until the sauce has reduced. Slice steak into thin strips. Serve immediately.

1 TEASPOON OLIVE OIL

¼ SMALL YELLOW ONION, FINELY CHOPPED

¼ POUND EYE ROUND STEAK, FAT TRIMMED

¼ CUP BEEF BROTH

1 TABLESPOON FAT-FREE SOUR CREAM

½ TEASPOON DIJON MUSTARD

½ TEASPOON SOY SAUCE

½ TEASPOON GARLIC POWDER

Quinoa and Beef–Stuffed Acorn Squash

YIELDS 2 SERVINGS

1. Preheat oven to 350°F. Remove the stem and cut the squash in half lengthwise. Use a spoon to remove the seeds and strings to create a hollow in each half. Sprinkle each half lightly with salt and pepper.

2. Place a small skillet over medium heat. Once it is warm, add the ground beef and stir continually with a fork, breaking the beef into small pieces. When cooked, drain off any excess grease and add the beef to a bowl with the pilaf. Stir to combine and place half of the mixture in each hollow of squash.

3. Pour half the vegetable broth and sprinkle half the cheese on each squash half. Place the squash in a small skillet in the middle of the oven for 40–50 minutes. It is ready when you can pierce the flesh with a fork through to the skin easily. Let each half cool for 5 minutes before serving.

1 ACORN SQUASH

PINCH SALT

PINCH PEPPER

2 OUNCES GROUND BEEF

1 SERVING QUINOA PILAF (CHAPTER 12)

¼ CUP VEGETABLE BROTH

2 TEASPOONS PARMESAN CHEESE

QUINOA AND BEEF-STUFFED ACORN SQUASH

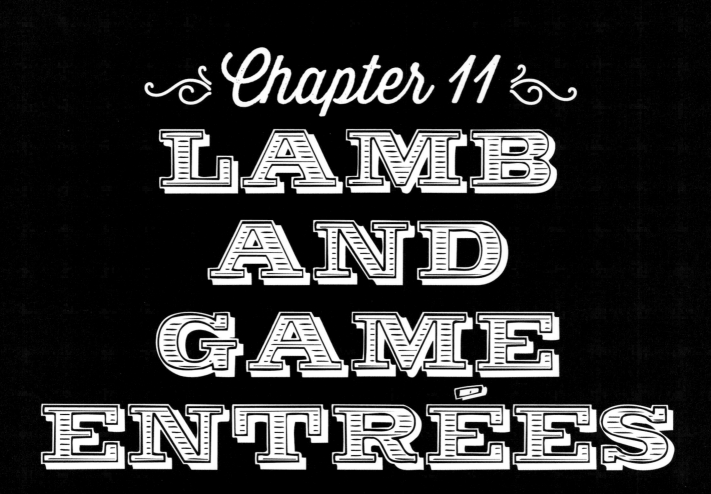

Chapter 11
LAMB AND GAME ENTRÉES

Seared Venison Steaks with Peppercorn Gin Sauce

YIELDS 4 SERVINGS

1. Place the venison steaks in a sealable plastic bag with the gin and the peppercorns. Let them sit at room temperature for at least 30 minutes or in the refrigerator for 2–24 hours.

2. Place a skillet over medium-high heat. Once it's heated, add the oil. Lay the steaks in the pan and cook for 2–4 minutes on each side.

3. Once the meat is cooked, remove it from the pan and keep warm. Add the gin and peppercorn sauce to the skillet with the Worcestershire and onion. Cook for 4–6 minutes. Pour the sauce over the steaks and serve while hot.

4 VENISON STEAKS, 4–6 OUNCES EACH

¼ CUP GIN

1 TEASPOON PEPPERCORNS

2 TABLESPOONS OLIVE OIL

2 TEASPOONS WORCESTERSHIRE SAUCE

1 ONION, CHOPPED

Stewed Lamb with Cilantro and Mint

1. Place a skillet over medium-high heat. Once it's heated, add the butter. When the butter has melted, add the lamb and cook for 10 minutes, turning the meat every 1–2 minutes until it's browned on all sides.

2. Remove the meat from the skillet and add the onion. Cook for 8–10 minutes. Add the tomatoes, tomato paste, and plums. Stir until everything is well coated. Stir in the chicken broth and the herbs. Add the lamb to the skillet, cover, reduce the heat to low, and simmer for 1 hour, or until the lamb is cooked through and soft. Stir in the lemon juice and then season to taste with salt and pepper.

3 TABLESPOONS BUTTER

2 POUNDS LAMB, CUT INTO 1" CUBES

1 LARGE ONION, CHOPPED

4 ROMA TOMATOES, CUBED

3 TABLESPOONS TOMATO PASTE

2 PLUMS, PITTED AND CHOPPED

3 CUPS CHICKEN BROTH

1 TABLESPOON CHOPPED DILL

1 TABLESPOON CHOPPED CILANTRO

1 TABLESPOON CHOPPED MINT

JUICE FROM 1 LEMON

SALT TO TASTE

PEPPER TO TASTE

Greek Lemon and Oregano Lamb

YIELDS 4 SERVINGS

1. Preheat oven to 350°F. Rinse and dry the lamb. Trim off any large pieces of fat or silverskin. Cut small slits into the meat and insert slivers of garlic. Mix the lemon juice, salt, pepper, and oregano in a small bowl. Rub the mixture over the lamb.

2. Place a skillet over medium-high heat. Once it's heated, add the lamb and sear it on each side for 4 minutes. Once it is browned, bake in the center of the oven for 1 hour.

3. Remove the pan from the oven and drain the fat. Rub the butter over the meat and return it to the skillet. Pour the water into the skillet and cook for 45 minutes. Toss the potatoes in the lemon zest and olive oil. Sprinkle liberally with salt and pepper and place around the lamb. Bake for 45–60 minutes, or until the potatoes and lamb are tender. Tent the skillet with foil and let it rest for 15 minutes before carving and serving.

2 POUNDS LAMB LEG ROAST, BONE IN

3 GARLIC CLOVES, SLICED

JUICE AND ZEST FROM 1 LEMON

1 TEASPOON SALT

½ TEASPOON GROUND BLACK PEPPER

2 TABLESPOONS DRIED OREGANO

2 TABLESPOONS BUTTER

1 CUP HOT WATER

1½ POUND POTATOES, SCRUBBED AND QUARTERED

2 TABLESPOONS OLIVE OIL

SALT TO TASTE

PEPPER TO TASTE

Cardamom and Ginger Lamb Curry

YIELDS 4–6 SERVINGS

1. Purée half the onion, the garlic, yogurt, and lemon juice in a blender.

2. Place a dry skillet over medium heat. Once it's heated, add the dry spices to the skillet and shake every few seconds. Cook for 2 minutes. Pour the spices into the blender with the olive oil and cornstarch and blend.

3. Pour the yogurt mixture over the lamb cubes in a sealable container. Toss so the meat is coated. Leave the meat at room temperature for 2 hours, or marinate overnight in the refrigerator.

4. Place a skillet over medium heat. Once it's heated, add the butter and vegetable oil. Mince the other half of the onion. Once the butter stops foaming, add the onion to the skillet. Cook for several minutes while stirring. Add the meat and the marinade and bring to a simmer. Add the whole cayenne pepper.

5. Reduce the heat to low and cover and simmer for 2 hours. Stir occasionally to keep the sauce from sticking. After 1 hour, taste the sauce. As soon as it seems hot enough, remove the pepper. Taste and season if needed.

1 SMALL YELLOW ONION, PEELED AND HALVED

1 SMALL GARLIC CLOVE

½ CUP GREEK-STYLE YOGURT

2 TEASPOONS LEMON JUICE

1 TEASPOON GROUND CORIANDER

½ TEASPOON SALT

½ TEASPOON CUMIN

½ TEASPOON GROUND CLOVES

½ TEASPOON GROUND CARDAMOM

½ TEASPOON BLACK PEPPER

¼ TEASPOON GROUND GINGER

¼ TEASPOON GROUND CINNAMON

½ TEASPOON OLIVE OIL

1½ TEASPOONS CORNSTARCH

1 POUND BONELESS LAMB, CUT INTO 1" CUBES

1 TABLESPOON BUTTER

1 TABLESPOON VEGETABLE OIL

1 CAYENNE PEPPER

CARDAMOM AND GINGER
LAMB CURRY

Herb-Roasted Rack of Lamb

YIELDS 4–6 SERVINGS

1. Trim all but a thin layer of fat from the lamb. Score the fat layer in a crosshatch pattern, being careful to not cut through to the meat. Combine the herbs and garlic in enough oil to coat the lamb. Sprinkle salt and pepper all over the meat and rub with the olive oil and herbs. Place in a container and seal tightly. Refrigerate for 8–24 hours.

2. Preheat oven to 425°F. Let the meat come to room temperature while the oven preheats.

3. Place a skillet over medium heat. Once it's heated add 2 tablespoons of oil. Place the lamb, fat-side down, in the skillet and cook for 6 minutes or until well browned. Repeat with the other rack. Remove the skillet from the heat.

4. Stand the racks in the skillet and lean them against each other with the fat side facing to the outside of the skillet.

5. Cook in the middle of the oven for 15 minutes. Reduce the heat to 325°F and roast for 5–15 minutes. Use a meat thermometer to test the meat's doneness: 130°F for medium-rare, 140°F for medium, and 150°F for well-done. Let it rest for 10 minutes before cutting the rack between the bones in sections of two and serve.

2 14–16-OUNCE RACKS OF LAMB

2 SPRIGS ROSEMARY, LEAVES STRIPPED AND CHOPPED

2 TABLESPOONS CHOPPED FRESH THYME

2 GARLIC CLOVES, MINCED

¼ CUP OLIVE OIL

SALT TO TASTE

PEPPER TO TASTE

Rustic Lamb and Spring Vegetable Stew

YIELDS 4 SERVINGS

1. Preheat oven to 350°F. Place a skillet over medium heat and add the oil and the onion. Cook for 8–10 minutes. Add the garlic and stir continually for 1 minute.

2. Season the lamb lightly with salt and pepper. Add the lamb cubes and cook for 2 minutes on each side, turning as needed, until all of the meat is browned.

3. Add the wine to the pan and scrape the bottom. Add the chicken stock, bay leaf, thyme, potatoes, carrots, and mush-rooms. Bring the contents to a boil and then cover the pan. Bake in the middle of the oven for 1 hour. Add the radishes to the pan, replace the lid, and bake for 30 minutes. Add the peas, replace the lid, and bake for 10 minutes. Remove the bay leaf and thyme sprig.

4. Season the broth with salt and pepper as needed and serve while warm with crusty bread.

2 TABLESPOONS OLIVE OIL

1 LARGE ONION, CHOPPED

1 GARLIC CLOVE, MINCED

1 POUND LEAN, BONELESS LAMB, CUT INTO CUBES

PINCH SALT

PINCH PEPPER

¼ CUP DRY WHITE WINE

4 CUPS CHICKEN STOCK

1 BAY LEAF

1 SPRIG FRESH THYME

2 POUNDS SMALL RED POTATOES, SCRUBBED

8 OUNCES BABY CARROTS

8 OUNCES BUTTON MUSHROOMS, HALVED

8 OUNCES RADISHES, STEMS AND ROOTS TRIMMED

8 OUNCES FROZEN PEAS

LAMB CHOPS WITH ROSEMARY AND WINE SAUCE

Lamb Chops with Rosemary and Wine Sauce

YIELDS 4 SERVINGS

1. Place a skillet over medium-high heat. Season the lamb chops with salt and pepper. Once the skillet is heated, add half of the oil and four of the chops. Cook on each side for 3 minutes. Remove them from the pan and keep warm. Repeat with the other four chops.

2. Pour off all but 1 tablespoon of the oil. Add the shallot to the pan and cook for 3–4 minutes, stirring frequently. Add the garlic and cook for 1 minute, stirring constantly.

3. Add the wine and scrape the bottom of the pan. Stir in the rosemary and increase the heat to high. Let the sauce boil for 3 minutes or until it has thickened to a syrup-like consistency.

4. Add the butter and stir until it melts. Sprinkle the flour over the pan and whisk it until it has thickened. Stir in the mustard and the sour cream. Return the chops to the pan and cook for 1–2 minutes. Taste the sauce and season with salt and pepper as necessary. Pour the sauce over the chops and serve while warm.

8 LAMB CHOPS

PINCH SALT

PINCH PEPPER

2 TABLESPOONS OLIVE OIL

1 SHALLOT, MINCED

1 CLOVE GARLIC, MINCED

1 CUP DRY RED WINE

1 TEASPOON FRESH ROSEMARY, MINCED

1 TEASPOON BUTTER

1 TEASPOON FLOUR

2 TABLESPOONS DIJON MUSTARD

3 TABLESPOONS SOUR CREAM

Lamb Shank with Swiss Chard

YIELDS 4 SERVINGS

1. Preheat oven to 300°F. Place a skillet over medium-high heat. Sprinkle the shanks with salt and pepper. Once the skillet is heated, add the oil and two shanks. Cook for 3–4 minutes on each side or until browned. Repeat with the remaining shanks.

2. Set aside the shanks. Add the onion, celery, and carrots to the pan and cook for 12–14 minutes. Pour the wine into the pan and scrape the bottom. Remove it from the heat and add the rosemary, bay leaves, and the lamb shanks. Fill the pan with chicken stock as necessary to cover all of the meat. Cook in the middle of the oven for 3 hours. Turn the shanks every 30 minutes.

3. Once the shanks are cooked, remove them from the pan and keep warm. Skim off some of the fat before placing the pan over a burner set to high heat. Boil until the sauce is reduced and thickened. Reduce the heat to low.

4. Wash the chard, cut out the stalk, and tear the leaves into large pieces. Add the chard to the sauce, place a cover on the pan, and cook for 2–3 minutes. Pour the sauce and chard over the meat and serve while warm.

4 LAMB SHANKS, 1" OF THE LOWER BONE EXPOSED

2 TEASPOONS SALT

1 TEASPOON GROUND PEPPER

2 TABLESPOONS VEGETABLE OIL

1 MEDIUM ONION, THINLY SLICED

2 CELERY STALKS, THINLY SLICED

2 CARROTS, THINLY SLICED

2 CUPS RED WINE

2 SPRIGS ROSEMARY

2 BAY LEAVES

1-2 CUPS CHICKEN STOCK

1 POUND SWISS CHARD

Skillet-Cooked Rabbit and Dumplings

YIELDS 4 SERVINGS

1. Place a large skillet over medium-high heat. Rinse the rabbit, pat dry, and add it to the pan with 1 tablespoon of the oil. Cook on each side for 3–4 minutes. Remove it from the pan.

2. Add the rest of the olive oil and ½ cup each of the onion, celery, and carrots to the skillet. Cook for 10–12 minutes, stirring frequently. Add half of the wine to the pan and scrape the bottom. Add the chicken stock. Return the rabbit to the pan. Reduce the heat to medium-low, cover, and simmer for 1 hour. Let the rabbit cool and remove the meat from the bones. Set aside with the broth and cooked vegetables.

3. Add 2 tablespoons of butter to the skillet over medium heat. Add the remaining onion, carrots, and celery with the turnip and celery root. Sprinkle with salt and sauté for 10 minutes. Add the herbs, garlic, and the rest of the wine, cooking and stirring continually until most of the wine evaporates. Preheat oven to 375°F.

4. Stir 1 tablespoon of butter into the skillet and add ¼ cup of the flour, stirring constantly. Cook for 5 minutes for a light roux or up to 15 minutes for a darker roux. Add reserved rabbit, vegetables, and broth. Whisk to prevent lumps from forming. Add salt, pepper, and Worcestershire sauce to taste. Leave on low heat.

5. Combine the remaining flour, ¼ teaspoon black pepper, ½ teaspoon salt, cayenne, nutmeg, and baking powder in a bowl. Combine melted butter, egg, and buttermilk into another bowl. Pour the dry ingredients into the wet and stir until the mixture just comes together.

6. Use a large spoon to drop dough into the bubbling mixture. Place the entire skillet in the middle of the oven and cook for 25–30 minutes. Serve warm.

1 RABBIT

3 TABLESPOONS OLIVE OIL

1 CUP CHOPPED WHITE ONION

1 CUP CHOPPED CELERY

1 CUP CHOPPED CARROT

1½ CUPS WHITE WINE

4 CUPS CHICKEN STOCK

3 TABLESPOONS BUTTER

½ CUP TURNIP, PEELED AND CHOPPED

½ CUP CELERY ROOT, PEELED AND CHOPPED

SALT TO TASTE

1 TABLESPOON FRESH ROSEMARY (1 TEASPOON DRIED)

3 TABLESPOONS FRESH THYME (1 TABLESPOON DRIED)

3 TABLESPOONS FRESH SAGE (1 TABLESPOON DRIED)

4 GARLIC CLOVES, MINCED

1½ CUPS ALL-PURPOSE FLOUR

PEPPER TO TASTE

1 TEASPOON WORCESTERSHIRE SAUCE

PINCH CAYENNE

PINCH GROUND NUTMEG

1 TABLESPOON BAKING POWDER

1 TABLESPOON MELTED BUTTER

1 EGG

½ CUP BUTTERMILK

Rabbit with Black Olives and Herbs

1. Preheat oven to 350°F. Rinse the rabbit pieces and pat dry. Season with salt and pepper. Dredge in flour and shake off any excess.

2. Place a skillet over medium-high heat. Once it's heated through, add 1 tablespoon of olive oil and half the rabbit pieces, meat-side down. Cook for 4–5 minutes. Remove them to a plate and repeat with the other pieces.

3. Add the remaining oil to the skillet with the onion, carrot, and celery. Cook for 8–10 minutes. Add the garlic and cook for 1 minute, stirring continually.

4. Add the chicken broth to the skillet and scrape the bottom of the pan. Stir in the olives, the herbs, and the rabbit pieces. Bake in the middle of the oven for 1 hour, or until the juices run clear when poked with a fork.

5. Remove the rabbit from the pan and keep it warm. Place the skillet over medium-high heat and boil until thickened. Pour the sauce over the rabbit and serve.

1 RABBIT, QUARTERED

SALT TO TASTE

PEPPER TO TASTE

½ CUP ALL-PURPOSE FLOUR

4 TABLESPOONS OLIVE OIL

1 SPANISH ONION, CHOPPED

1 CARROT, PEELED AND CHOPPED

1 CELERY STALK, CHOPPED

6 GARLIC CLOVES, CHOPPED

½ CUP CHICKEN BROTH

¾ CUP BLACK OLIVES, PITTED AND CHOPPED

2 TABLESPOONS FRESH THYME, CHOPPED

1 TABLESPOON FRESH OREGANO, CHOPPED

1 TABLESPOON FRESH BASIL, CHOPPED

Buffalo Steaks with Mushrooms and Green Onions

YIELDS 4 SERVINGS

1. Place steaks, 2 tablespoons oil, salt, vegetables, herbs, garlic, peppercorns, and lime in a sealable plastic bag. Remove as much of the air as possible and make sure the meat is evenly coated. Place in the refrigerator to marinate for 2–24 hours.

2. Place the bacon in a skillet over medium heat and cook for 5 minutes until crispy. Remove from the skillet and place on paper towels to drain.

3. Add the butter and mushrooms to the skillet. Cook for 5–7 minutes. Move the mushrooms to the outside of the skillet and place the scallions in the center. Cook for 2–3 minutes. Remove the mushrooms and scallions from the skillet.

4. Add 1 tablespoon olive oil to the skillet. Sprinkle the steaks with salt and pepper on each side. Cook the steaks on each side for 4–6 minutes. Remove the steaks and keep warm.

5. Place the marinade in the pan and boil for 3–4 minutes. Add the mushrooms and bacon and cook for another 2–3 minutes or until thickened. Pour some of the sauce over each steak and garnish with the fried scallions.

4 6-8-OUNCE RIBEYE BUFFALO STEAKS

3 TABLESPOONS OLIVE OIL

1 TEASPOON SALT

½ ONION, ROUGHLY CHOPPED

1 CARROT, ROUGHLY CHOPPED

1 CELERY STALK, ROUGHLY CHOPPED

1 TABLESPOON FRESH THYME

2 BAY LEAVES

3 GARLIC CLOVES, SMASHED

8 PEPPERCORNS, CRUSHED

JUICE AND ZEST OF 1 LIME

3 SLICES BACON, CUT INTO 1" SLICES

1 TABLESPOON BUTTER

4 OUNCES BUTTON MUSHROOMS, SLICED

4 SCALLIONS, OUTER LEAVES REMOVED, CUT LENGTHWISE

¼ TEASPOON GROUND BLACK PEPPER

Marjoram and Almond-Stuffed Venison Rolls

YIELDS 4–6 SERVINGS

1. Grate the zest from each piece of fruit into a small saucepan. Add the juice from the fruits to the pan with the chicken stock, orange juice, wine, and honey. Simmer over medium-high heat for 20 minutes. Remove it from the heat and cover.

2. Preheat oven to 400°F. Use a knife to slice halfway through each loin. Open each loin like a book. Sprinkle both sides with salt and pepper. Rub the inside with olive oil and sprinkle with marjoram. Keep them closed with twine or toothpicks.

3. Place a skillet over medium-high heat. Add the butter and sear each tenderloin for 1 minute on each side. Remove from the heat and bake in the oven for 5–10 minutes, or until the meat registers 125°F for medium-rare, 135°F for medium, or 145°F for medium-well.

4. Cover the tenderloins and let them rest for 10 minutes. Place the saucepan over medium heat. Stir in the almonds. Remove from the heat when the sauce starts to bubble. Slice the tenderloin into ½" rounds and spoon the almond citrus mixture over each one. Serve while warm.

1 ORANGE

1 LEMON

1 LIME

½ CUP CHICKEN STOCK

1 CUP ORANGE JUICE

½ CUP PORT OR DRY RED WINE

1 TABLESPOON HONEY

2 1-POUND VENISON TENDERLOINS

SALT TO TASTE

PEPPER TO TASTE

1 TABLESPOON OLIVE OIL

4 SPRIGS MARJORAM OR OREGANO, LEAVES REMOVED AND CHOPPED

2 TABLESPOONS BUTTER

½ POUND WHOLE ALMONDS

Ostrich Scallopine with Peppercorn Crust

YIELDS 2 SERVINGS

1. Rinse the ostrich and pat dry. Place the steaks between two layers of plastic wrap and beat them with a rolling pin until they're no more than ½" thick. Sprinkle each side of the steaks with salt and pepper. Sprinkle a pinch of crushed peppercorns on each side and press into the meat.

2. Place a skillet over medium-high heat. Once it's heated through, add the oil and the steaks. Cook the steaks on each side for 1½–2 minutes. Remove them from the skillet and let rest for 10 minutes before serving.

3. Add the vinegar to the skillet and scrape the bottom. Add the butter and let it melt. Once it has melted, add the shallot, stirring continually for 2 minutes. Pour the shallot and vinegar mixture over the steaks and serve while they're hot.

2 4-OUNCE OSTRICH STEAKS

SALT TO TASTE

PEPPER TO TASTE

20 PEPPERCORNS, CRUSHED

1 TABLESPOON OLIVE OIL

3 TABLESPOONS BALSAMIC VINEGAR

1 TABLESPOON BUTTER

1 SHALLOT MINCED

Japanese Braised Boar on Soba Noodles

1. Preheat oven to 275°F. Sprinkle salt and pepper on the boar. Place a skillet over medium-high heat. Once it's heated, add the peanut oil. Sear the meat on each side for 3 minutes, or until it is browned. Remove the meat from the pan.

2. Add the sake to the pan and use a spoon to scrape any stuck-on bits. Stir in the ginger, stock, honey, soy sauce, and Szechuan pepper. Place the meat back in the pan and let the sauce come to a boil.

3. Cover and cook in the center of the oven for 3–4 hours, or until the meat is tender and close to falling apart. Remove it from the skillet and keep warm.

4. Place the skillet over medium heat and let the sauce boil until it reduces by half. Cook the soba noodles according to the package directions. Slice the meat thinly and serve it on the soba noodles. Pour some of the pan reduction over the noodles and sprinkle with scallion. Serve warm.

SALT TO TASTE

PEPPER TO TASTE

1½ POUNDS BOAR SHOULDER

1 TABLESPOON PEANUT OIL

¼ CUP SAKE

1 THUMB-SIZED PIECE FRESH GINGER, PEELED AND MATCHSTICKED

3 CUPS VEGETABLE STOCK

1 TEASPOON HONEY

1 TABLESPOON SOY SAUCE

⅛ TEASPOON GROUND SZECHUAN PEPPER

1 POUND DRY SOBA NOODLES

1 SCALLION, THINLY SLICED

Wild Boar Ragu

YIELDS 6 SERVINGS

1. Use paper towels to pat dry the meat. Sprinkle with salt, pepper, and garlic powder.

2. Place a Dutch oven over medium heat. Once it's heated, add the oil and one layer of meat. Cook for 3–4 minutes on each side, turning as needed. Remove from the pan once they're seared all over and repeat with the remaining meat.

3. Remove the last batch of meat from the pan, add more oil if necessary, and add the onion and fennel. Cook for 10–12 minutes. Add the garlic and stir continually for 1 minute. Stir in the red wine and scrape the bottom of the pan.

4. Crush the tomatoes and add them with the liquid. Add 1 can of water. Add the oregano and more pepper if desired. Return the meat to the pan and reduce the heat to low. Cover and cook for 1½–2 hours. Stir occasionally. Serve over pasta or polenta.

2 POUNDS BONELESS WILD BOAR SHOULDER, CUT INTO 1" CUBES

2 TABLESPOONS SALT

1 TEASPOON GROUND BLACK PEPPER

1 TABLESPOON GARLIC POWDER

2 TABLESPOONS OLIVE OIL

1 LARGE ONION, DICED

1 FENNEL BULB, DICED

8 GARLIC CLOVES, DICED

1 CUP DRY RED WINE

2 28-OUNCE CANS WHOLE TOMATOES

2 TABLESPOONS DRIED OREGANO

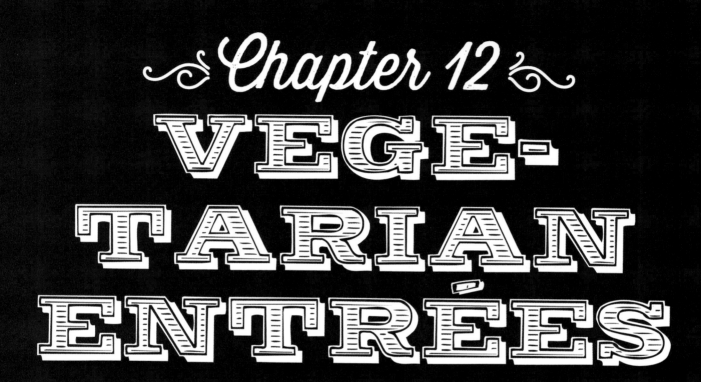

Chapter 12
VEGE-TARIAN ENTRÉES

Griddle Quesadilla with Chipotle and Black Beans

YIELDS 4 SERVINGS

1. Place the beans in a bowl and mash them with a fork. Stir in the chipotle and tomato.

2. Place a griddle over medium heat. Once it's heated, place two tortillas on the griddle. Don't overlap them. Sprinkle ¼ cup of cheese on each tortilla. Spoon ¼ of the bean mixture on top of the cheese. Top with another tortilla and press down slightly.

3. Cook for 4–6 minutes on the first side, or until the tortilla is slightly browned. Press the top tortilla to make it stick to the cheese. Carefully flip the tortilla.

4. Cook on the second side for 4–6 minutes, or until the tortilla is slightly browned. Repeat for remaining tortillas. Cut into wedges and serve with salsa and sour cream.

1 15-OUNCE CAN BLACK BEANS, DRAINED AND RINSED

2 TABLESPOONS CANNED CHIPOTLE

1 CUP DICED TOMATO, SEEDED

8 FLOUR OR CORN TORTILLAS

1 CUP SHREDDED CHEESE

Baked Barley Risotto with Mushrooms, Onions, and Carrots

YIELDS 6–8 SERVINGS

1. Preheat oven to 350°F. Place a Dutch oven over medium heat and add the oil, carrots, and onion once heated. Stir frequently and cook until the onion is brown and the carrots are soft. Add the mushrooms and sauté for 10 minutes.

2. Increase the heat slightly and add the wine, thyme, and barley. Stir continually until the wine is evaporated, 3–4 minutes. Add the broth and boil.

3. Turn off the heat and cover. Cook in the middle of the oven for 50–60 minutes. Stir frequently until the liquid is absorbed and the barley is tender. Stir in the parsley and cheese. Taste before adding salt and pepper.

1 TABLESPOON OLIVE OIL

3 CARROTS, CHOPPED

1 MEDIUM YELLOW ONION, CHOPPED

8 OUNCES WHITE MUSHROOMS, SLICED

½ CUP WHITE WINE OR VERMOUTH

1½ TEASPOONS DRIED THYME

2 CUPS BARLEY

4 CUPS CHICKEN OR VEGETABLE BROTH

3 TABLESPOONS FRESH PARSLEY

½ CUP GRATED PARMESAN CHEESE

SALT TO TASTE

PEPPER TO TASTE

BAKED BARLEY RISOTTO WITH MUSHROOMS, ONIONS, AND CARROTS

Plantain Empanadas with Queso Fresco

YIELDS 12 EMPANADAS

1. Preheat oven to 350°F. Cut the ends off the unpeeled plantains and then cut them in half lengthwise. Cook on a baking sheet for 40 minutes; they should be very soft. Allow them to cool until they can be handled, then remove the peel. Place the soft plantain into a food processor with the salt and garlic. Pulse several times until smooth. Add half the flour and pulse. Add the remainder of the flour and pulse until all of the flour is incorporated. Scrape down the sides of the bowl to get an even dough.

2. Prepare your work area by filling half a medium bowl with cold water. Tear three square sheets of wax paper. Set one of them aside for holding the empanadas before they're fried. Keep your hands wet at all times. Dip your palms into the water and divide the dough into twelve equal portions. Lightly wet one side of each piece of wax paper.

3. Place one of the dough balls onto the wet side of one piece of wax paper. Place the wet side of the other sheet on top. Lightly press down on the ball until you get a circle slightly larger than your palm. Carefully peel off the top piece of wax paper. Place a tablespoon of crumbled queso fresco into the center of the circle. Hold the wax paper in your hand and fold it to get even sides. Carefully peel the paper away from the empanada and use the tines of a fork to press the edges together. Set the empanada aside and repeat.

4. Place a fryer over medium-high heat. The oil should be 350°F. Fry two empanadas at a time. They should be golden brown after 1 minute on each side. Place on a rack to drain over paper towels. Sprinkle with coarse salt. Serve warm with salsa.

2 LARGE YELLOW-RIPE PLANTAINS

¾ TABLESPOON SALT

1 LARGE GARLIC CLOVE

1 CUP ALL-PURPOSE FLOUR

WATER, AS NEEDED

1½ CUPS QUESO FRESCO

VEGETABLE OIL, AS NEEDED

Grill Pan Dijon Tomatoes

YIELDS 2 SERVINGS

1. Preheat broiler on high and place a grill pan in the middle of the oven. In a small bowl, combine the mustard, salt, pepper, butter, bread crumbs, and Parmesan cheese.

2. Once the grill pan is hot, brush the cut side of each tomato lightly with the oil and place cut-side down. Cook for 2–3 minutes. If the skin on the uncut side starts to blacken, remove tomatoes from the oven.

3. Carefully turn the tomato halves over. Place a quarter of the mustard mixture onto each tomato half and sprinkle lightly with paprika. Return the skillet to the oven and cook for 3–5 minutes until the mustard mixture is golden brown. Serve immediately.

1 TABLESPOON DIJON MUSTARD

1 TEASPOON SALT

LARGE PINCH BLACK PEPPER

3 TABLESPOONS MELTED BUTTER

¼ CUP PANKO BREAD CRUMBS

¼ CUP PARMESAN CHEESE, SHREDDED

2 MEDIUM TOMATOES, CUT IN HALF LENGTHWISE AND SEEDED

1 TEASPOON OLIVE OR VEGETABLE OIL

PAPRIKA TO TASTE

GRILLED ARTICHOKES

Grilled Artichokes

YIELDS 2 SERVINGS

1. Add 1" of water to a pot large enough to hold the artichokes and place over medium heat. Add the lemon juice and lemon halves. Cover and bring to a boil.

2. Remove the outer ring of lower leaves. Cut off the tips of each artichoke leaf to remove the barb. Cut off the top inch of the artichoke and the last inch of the stem.

3. Place the artichokes in the water with the stem up. Reduce the heat to low, cover, and steam for 15 minutes. Remove them from the pan. Discard the water and lemon. Place the chokes on a cutting board, top down. Slice the artichoke in half. Use a melon baller or spoon to remove the fuzzy choke.

4. Place a grill pan over medium-high heat. Once it's heated, brush the olive oil on the cut side of the artichokes and sprinkle lightly with salt and pepper. Place the chokes cut-side down on the grill pan and cook for 10 minutes. Turn them a quarter turn after cooking for 5 minutes. Serve with a garlic mayonnaise.

WATER, AS NEEDED

1 LEMON, JUICED

2 LARGE ARTICHOKES

1 TABLESPOON OLIVE OIL

SALT TO TASTE

PEPPER TO TASTE

Artisinal Grilled Vegetables

YIELDS 2 SERVINGS

1. Trim the bottoms off the asparagus. Cut thick stalks in half lengthwise. Slice the button mushrooms in half through the stem.

2. Cut the zucchini in half lengthwise and then into ½" slices. Place on top of two layers of paper towels. Sprinkle lightly with salt. Let sit for 10 minutes. Flip over, sprinkle with salt, and let sit for another 10 minutes.

3. Remove the stems and seeds from the peppers. Cut in half and make small cuts as needed in the bottom of the peppers so they will lie flat.

4. Cut the stems off the eggplants, then cut ½" slices along their length. Cut in half lengthwise if desired. Salt the same way as the zucchini, but let rest for 20 minutes on each side.

5. Place a griddle over medium-high heat on a stovetop. Toss the asparagus and mushrooms in a tablespoon of olive oil separately. Sprinkle them lightly with salt and pepper. Brush the grill lightly with oil. Cook the asparagus for 2–4 minutes on each side. Place them on a warmed platter.

6. Cook the mushrooms for 2–4 minutes on each side and add them to the platter. Pat the eggplant and zucchini dry and place several slices on the pan. Cook for 4–6 minutes on each side. Place them on the platter.

7. Brush both sides of the peppers with oil. Place them on the pan skin-side up. Grill for 2–4 minutes on each side. Sprinkle with salt and pepper and add to the platter. Keep the platter warm until ready to serve.

2 BUNCHES ASPARAGUS

16 OUNCES BUTTON MUSHROOMS

3 ZUCCHINIS

SALT TO TASTE

6 CUBANELLE PEPPERS

2 EGGPLANTS

¼ CUP OLIVE OIL

PEPPER TO TASTE

Vegetable Green Curry

YIELDS 4 SERVINGS

1. Place a skillet over medium heat. Once it is heated, add the curry paste and the vegetable broth and stir to combine.

2. Stir in the sweet potato cubes, cover, and cook for 15–20 minutes, or until you can pierce them with a fork. Stir the contents occasionally to keep them from sticking.

3. Turn up the heat to medium-high and remove the lid. Add the remaining vegetables and cook for 5–7 minutes, stirring frequently.

4. Once the liquid has reduced, lower the heat to medium-low and add the lime juice and coconut milk. Keep the coconut milk from boiling and cook for 2–3 minutes. Serve in bowls with cooked white rice.

¼ CUP GREEN CURRY PASTE (CHAPTER 6)

2 CUPS VEGETABLE BROTH

1 LARGE SWEET POTATO, PEELED AND CUT INTO ½" CUBES

¼ POUND GREEN BEANS, STEMS REMOVED

8 OUNCES SLICED BUTTON MUSHROOMS

8 OUNCES FRESH SPINACH LEAVES

JUICE FROM 1 LIME

1 CAN COCONUT MILK

Quinoa Pilaf

YIELDS 2 SERVINGS

1. Place a skillet over medium heat and when warm add the olive oil and onion. Cook for 5–7 minutes, stirring occasionally. The onion should be soft and just starting to turn golden. Add the cinnamon, coriander, turmeric, and chili flakes. Stir continually for 1 minute and then add the vegetable broth.

2. Use your spatula to loosen any spices or onion that may have stuck to the skillet. Add the garlic, quinoa, and beans. Reduce the heat to low, cover the skillet, and simmer for 15 minutes. The water should be mostly absorbed.

3. Add the tomato, olives, and dried fruit. Stir and cook for 5 more minutes, or until the water is evaporated. Fluff with a fork and serve immediately.

1 TABLESPOON OLIVE OIL

½ SMALL ONION, CHOPPED

¼ TEASPOON GROUND CINNAMON

½ TEASPOON GROUND CORIANDER

½ TEASPOON GROUND TURMERIC

PINCH RED CHILI FLAKES

1 CUP VEGETABLE BROTH

1 SMALL GARLIC CLOVE, MINCED

½ CUP QUINOA

½ CAN RED KIDNEY BEANS, RINSED AND DRAINED

1 ROMA TOMATO, CHOPPED

6 OLIVES, CHOPPED

2 TABLESPOONS DRIED CURRANTS OR CRANBERRIES

Skillet-Cooked Migas

YIELDS 1 SERVING

1. Place skillet over medium heat.

2. Crack the eggs into a small bowl and mix in the salsa and water. Set aside.

3. Once the skillet is heated, add the butter and olive oil. Once the foaming stops, tear up 2 corn tortillas and sauté them until they're soft. Add the onion to the skillet. Cook and stir for 5 minutes, or until the onion is translucent and soft. Stir in the green chilies.

4. Pour the egg mixture in the skillet and slowly fold until the eggs are cooked through. Sprinkle the tomato over the top of the eggs.

5. Remove the skillet from the heat and stir in the avocado, cilantro, and cheese. Turn out onto a plate and serve with sour cream and warmed corn tortillas.

2 LARGE EGGS

1 TABLESPOON CHUNKY SALSA

1 TEASPOON WATER

1 TABLESPOON BUTTER

1 TABLESPOON OLIVE OIL

4 6" CORN TORTILLAS

¼ SMALL ONION, FINELY CHOPPED

2 TABLESPOONS CHOPPED GREEN CHILIES

½ SMALL TOMATO, CHOPPED

½ AVOCADO, SLICED

1 TEASPOON FRESH CILANTRO

3 TABLESPOONS GRATED MONTEREY JACK CHEESE

DOLLOP SOUR CREAM

ASPARAGUS AND LEEK FRITTATA

Asparagus and Leek Frittata

YIELDS 1 SERVING

1. Steam the piece of asparagus if it isn't already cooked. Place a skillet over medium heat. Once it is warm, add the butter and the leeks. Cook the leeks slowly and stir frequently for 8–10 minutes. Add the asparagus to the skillet.

2. Turn on the broiler. In a separate bowl, whisk together the eggs, cheese, chives, salt, and pepper. Once the leeks are soft and the asparagus is warmed, pour the egg mixture into the skillet. Let the eggs cook for 5–6 minutes without stirring.

3. Once the bottom and sides of the eggs are firm, add the tomato slices to the top of the frittata, then place the skillet under the broiler about 4" from the heat. Let the frittata cook until the top of the eggs are lightly browned, about 4–5 minutes.

4. Remove the pan from the oven and while it is still hot, run a thin knife along the edges of the skillet to loosen the frittata. Slide the frittata onto a plate and serve immediately.

1 STALK COOKED ASPARAGUS, CHOPPED

1 TEASPOON UNSALTED BUTTER

¼ CUP CHOPPED LEEKS

2 LARGE EGGS

2 TABLESPOONS PARMESAN CHEESE, SHREDDED

2 TABLESPOONS GRUYÈRE, SHREDDED

1 TEASPOON CHIVES, MINCED

PINCH SALT

PINCH PEPPER

1 ROMA TOMATO, SLICED

Leek, Mushroom, and Goat Cheese Quesadilla

YIELDS 1 SERVING

1. Place a small skillet over medium heat. Once heated, add 1 tablespoon olive oil and the leek. Cook for 3–4 minutes, or until the leek is just starting to soften. Add the mushrooms, garlic powder, and salt and pepper to taste and stir frequently for 4–5 minutes. The mushrooms should reduce and the leeks should start to turn golden.

2. Remove the contents of the skillet to a small bowl. Wipe out the skillet and add 1 teaspoon of olive oil. Place one corn tortilla in the skillet and add the leek and mushroom mixture on top of it. Add the cheese on top, being careful to keep it from touching the sides of the skillet. Place another tortilla on top and press down.

3. Cook for 3–4 minutes, or until the bottom tortilla is crispy. Carefully remove the quesadilla from the skillet and flip over. Cook the second side for 2–3 minutes or until crispy.

4. Remove from skillet and let it rest for 3 minutes before slicing in half and serving with or without salsa and sour cream.

1 TABLESPOON PLUS 1 TEASPOON OLIVE OIL

¼ CUP LEEK, CHOPPED

¼ CUP MUSHROOMS, CHOPPED

½ TEASPOON GARLIC POWDER

SALT TO TASTE

PEPPER TO TASTE

2 CORN TORTILLAS

¼ CUP GOAT CHEESE, CRUMBLED

½ CUP SALSA AND SOUR CREAM (OPTIONAL)

LEEK, MUSHROOM, AND GOAT CHEESE QUESADILLA

Tofu Steak with Mushrooms

YIELDS 1 SERVING

1. Place the tofu in the microwave for 1 minute. Drain off the water and cut the block into 4 even slices.

2. Combine the soy sauce, sesame oil, rice wine vinegar, and hot sauce in a small bowl. Place the drained tofu steak in the sauce and let it rest in the refrigerator for 1–24 hours.

3. Place a small skillet over medium heat. Once it is heated, add 1 tablespoon of the oil and the mushrooms. Sprinkle the salt over the mushrooms and toss to combine. Cook for 4 minutes.

4. Remove the mushrooms from the skillet and add the remaining oil. Remove the tofu from the marinade and place it in the skillet. Cook on each side for 2 minutes.

5. Return the mushrooms to the skillet. Pour the marinade over the steak and cook until the mushrooms have warmed and the sauce has reduced. Sprinkle with chopped scallion and serve while warm.

¼ POUND FIRM TOFU STEAK, PRESSED

2 TABLESPOONS SOY SAUCE

1 TEASPOON TOASTED SESAME OIL

1 TABLESPOON RICE WINE VINEGAR

SEVERAL DASHES HOT SAUCE

2 TABLESPOONS PEANUT OR OLIVE OIL

¼ CUP MUSHROOMS, SLICED

¼ TEASPOON SALT

1 GREEN SCALLION, THINLY SLICED

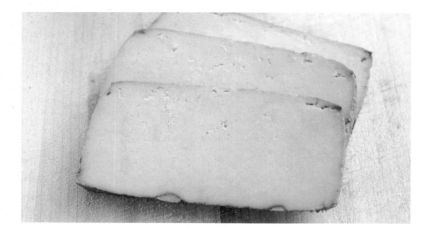

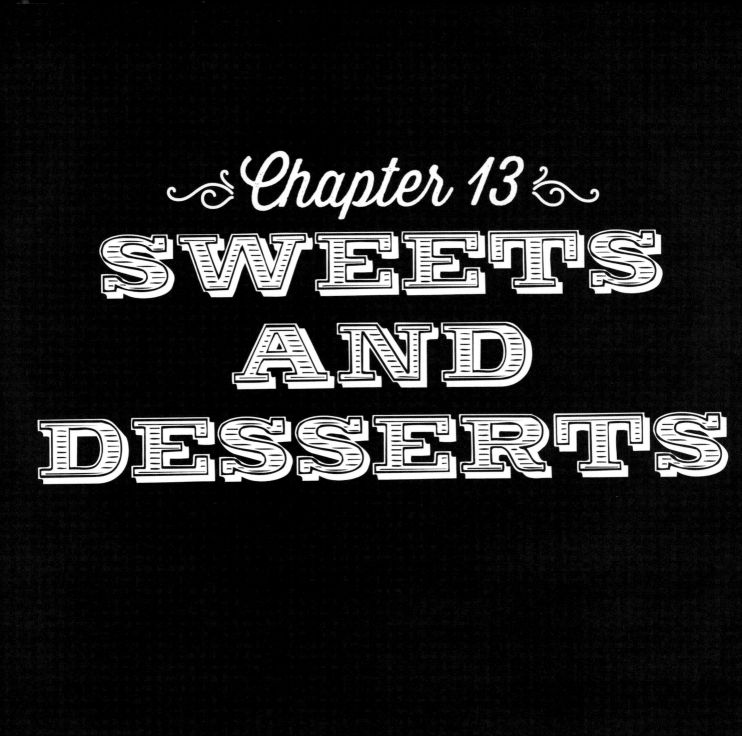

Chapter 13
SWEETS AND DESSERTS

Crushed Almond Shortbread Cookies

YIELDS 2 DOZEN COOKIES

1. Preheat oven to 350°F. Using the paddle attachment on a stand mixer or hand mixer, cream the butter and sugar together. Add the extracts and combine.

2. Sift the flour and salt together. Stir the crushed almonds into the flour. Slowly add the flour to the butter while mixing slowly. When mixed, turn onto a floured surface and shape into a flat disk. Refrigerate for 1 hour.

3. Flour a surface and roll the dough until it is ½" thick. Cut into rounds or squares that are no larger than 2½" across. Place 1 whole almond on the top of each cookie, if desired. Place the cookies on a griddle and bake in the middle of the oven for 20–25 minutes. The edges will turn brown. Cool to room temperature and serve.

3 STICKS UNSALTED BUTTER, AT ROOM TEMPERATURE

1 CUP GRANULATED SUGAR

1 TEASPOON VANILLA EXTRACT

1 TEASPOON ALMOND EXTRACT

3½ CUPS ALL-PURPOSE FLOUR

¼ TEASPOON SALT

1½ CUPS CRUSHED ALMONDS

24 WHOLE ALMONDS, OPTIONAL

CRUSHED ALMOND SHORTBREAD COOKIES

Griddle-Baked Scones

1. Preheat oven to 400°F and place a griddle on a rack in the middle of the oven. Mix the flour, baking powder, sugar, and salt either in a food processor or by hand until well combined.

2. Add the butter and mix until it is coarse crumbs with a few larger chunks of butter, 12–14 pulses if using a food processor. Add the fruit or nuts and pulse quickly until combined.

3. Use a rubber spatula to stir in the cream and egg until a dough starts to form. Dump the mixture onto a floured surface and knead until it has come together but has a rough and sticky texture.

4. Pat the dough into a circle and use a sharp knife to cut it into eight triangular wedges. Place on the griddle and bake for 12–15 minutes. The tops should be golden brown when ready. Cool for 10 minutes before serving with butter, jam, or clotted cream.

2 CUPS ALL-PURPOSE FLOUR

1 TABLESPOON BAKING POWDER

3 TABLESPOONS SUGAR

¾ TEASPOON SALT

4 TABLESPOONS BUTTER, COLD AND CUBED

½ CUP DRIED FRUIT OR NUTS, CHOPPED

¾ CUP HEAVY CREAM

1 LARGE EGG, LIGHTLY BEATEN

Cinnamon Welshcakes

YIELDS 20 CAKES

1. Cut the cold butter into the flour until it's a crumbly mix. Stir in ¼ cup of sugar and spices. Add the egg to make a dough that is soft but not sticky. If the dough is sticky, add a tablespoon or two of flour.

2. Shape the dough into a disc, cover it with plastic wrap, and refrigerate for at least 30 minutes.

3. Flour a surface and roll the dough until it is ¼" thick. Use a biscuit cutter to make small cakes. Re-roll the scrap and cut more biscuits until you have used all the dough.

4. Place a griddle over medium heat. Once it's heated, grease the pan lightly with the butter or oil. Add a few of the cakes and cook on each side for 3 minutes until golden brown. Keep them warm and sprinkle them with the remaining sugar. Serve while warm.

½ CUP COLD BUTTER, DICED

1⅔ CUPS SELF-RISING CAKE FLOUR

¼ CUP PLUS 2 TABLESPOONS SUGAR

¼ TEASPOON ALLSPICE

¼ TEASPOON CINNAMON

1 LARGE EGG, BEATEN

1 TABLESPOON BUTTER OR VEGETABLE OIL

Bread Pudding with Cinnamon and Vanilla

YIELDS 1 LOAF OR 12 MUFFINS

1. Preheat oven to 350°F. Place a loaf pan or muffin pans on the middle rack.

2. Add the melted butter to a large mixing bowl. Whisk in the brown sugar, vanilla extract, ground cinnamon, milk, and eggs. Add the bread cubes to the bowl and press lightly till they have soaked up all of the liquid.

3. Pour the contents into a loaf pan and use a spoon to spread out. Bake for 40 minutes. Or fill the muffin cups about two-thirds with the mix and bake for 30 minutes.

4. Let the pans rest for 10 minutes before running a knife along the outside edge to help dislodge the contents.

2 TABLESPOONS BUTTER, MELTED

¼ CUP PACKED BROWN SUGAR

1 TEASPOON VANILLA EXTRACT

1 TEASPOON GROUND CINNAMON

½ CUP WHOLE MILK

3 EGGS

6 SLICES BREAD, CUBED

Cherry Almond Cake

YIELDS 1 LOAF CAKE

1. Preheat oven to 325°F. Pit the cherries and cut in half. Place them on a plate and sprinkle with flour. Toss to coat them evenly and shake to remove the excess.

2. Place the butter and sugar in a mixer bowl and beat until light and fluffy. Add the eggs gradually until well blended. Add the almond extract and combine.

3. Combine the cake flour and almonds. Sprinkle the flour mixture over the wet ingredients and fold in the flour gently. Fold in the cherries and milk.

4. Once the liquid is combined, pour into the loaf pan and bake for 45–60 minutes, or until an inserted toothpick comes out clean.

1 CUP FRESH CHERRIES

¼ CUP ALL-PURPOSE FLOUR

1 CUP BUTTER, SOFTENED

½ CUP AND 1 TABLESPOON SUGAR

3 LARGE EGGS, BEATEN

¼ TEASPOON ALMOND EXTRACT

1⅔ CUPS SELF-RISING CAKE FLOUR

½ CUP FINELY CHOPPED ALMONDS

⅓ CUP MILK

Buttered Rum Pineapple

1. Place a skillet over medium heat. Once it is heated through, add the brown sugar, rum, and butter and stir until the butter is melted and bubbling.

2. Place the pineapple slices in the skillet one at a time and cook for 3 minutes or until they're warmed through. Serve while hot.

½ CUP BROWN SUGAR

¼ CUP DARK RUM

3 TABLESPOONS BUTTER

1 PINEAPPLE, CORED AND CUT INTO ½" SLICES

Garbanzo Bean Brownies

1. Place a skillet in the middle of the oven and preheat to 350°F. Place eggs in a food processor with garbanzo beans. Purée until very smooth. It should have air bubbles, but stop before it starts to look like a meringue.

2. Melt the chocolate chips in a double boiler or microwave. Add a few tablespoons of chocolate to the processor and pulse. Then slowly pour in the rest of the chocolate. Scrape down the sides as necessary.

3. Once the mixture is a uniform color, add sugar and vanilla. Purée 1 minute. Add flour and baking powder. Purée until incorporated. Pour mixture into a skillet and bake 1 hour. Cool 5 minutes before turning out and cutting.

4 EGGS

1 CAN GARBANZO BEANS, DRAINED

1½ CUPS CHOCOLATE CHIPS

1¼ CUPS SUGAR

1 TABLESPOON VANILLA

¼ CUP CHICKPEA FLOUR

¾ TEASPOON BAKING POWDER

GARBANZO BEAN BROWNIES

Ebelskiver

1. Separate the egg whites from the yolks and place into two bowls. Whip the whites to a stiff peak. Beat the yolks with the sugar, butter, milks, salt, and vanilla. Sift the flour, baking soda, and baking powder together. Stir it into the egg yolk mixture. Fold in the egg whites.

2. Place the ebelskiver pan over medium heat and let it warm for several minutes. Use a basting brush to brush the depressions with oil. Once the pan is hot, fill the depressions halfway with batter. Place ½ teaspoon syrup in the center of the depression and cover with more batter if necessary. Cook for 1–2 minutes on the first side or until there are visible bubbles and the surface starts to look dry.

3. Use a skewer or a crochet hook to lightly pierce the cooked edge of the batter and flip it upside down. Repeat in the same order the depressions were filled. Cook for 1 minute before removing. Oil the depressions again and repeat until all the batter has been used. Serve warm.

3 EGGS

2 TABLESPOONS SUGAR

3 TABLESPOONS MELTED BUTTER

1½ CUPS BUTTERMILK

½ CUP MILK

½ TEASPOON SALT

1 TEASPOON VANILLA EXTRACT

2 CUPS FLOUR

1 TEASPOON BAKING SODA

1 TEASPOON BAKING POWDER

2 TABLESPOONS CANOLA OR VEGETABLE OIL

¼ CUP FRUIT SYRUP OR ½ CUP COOKED FRUIT CHUNKS

Sweet and Savory Apple Foldover

YIELDS 8 SERVINGS

1. Place the flour, cornmeal, and 3 tablespoons sugar in a food processor and pulse several times. Add half of the butter and pulse 8–10 times to get even-sized lumps. Add the rest of the butter and repeat. Spray the top of the flour with water until it is evenly dampened. Pulse three times, wait 30 seconds, and pulse three more times. Press on the dough. It should come together. Repeat the spraying if it doesn't.

2. Pour the dough into a large sealable bag and mold into a disk. Refrigerate for 30 minutes.

3. Preheat oven to 400°F. Place a skillet over medium heat. When warm, add the apples and toss for 30 seconds. Add the vinegar. Stir for 30 seconds or until the vinegar evaporates. Add ¼ cup sugar and toss to combine. Cook for 2–3 minutes, or until the apples start to soften.

4. Remove the skillet from the heat and add the spices and 2 tablespoons butter. Stir until the butter has melted and coats the apple. Stir in the cheese. Cool apples in a bowl to room temperature. Clean the skillet.

5. Place the dough between two sheets of wax paper. Roll until it is about ¼" thick. Slide the dough into the skillet. Pile the apple mixture onto the center, leaving about 2" of crust on all sides. Sprinkle the apples with flour. Fold the extra crust toward the center and pinch where the edges meet.

6. Brush the top of the crust with the egg white and sprinkle with 1 tablespoon of sugar. Bake in the center of the oven for 30 minutes. The crust should be golden brown. Let the pie rest for about 20 minutes before serving.

2½ CUPS ALL-PURPOSE FLOUR

½ CUP CORNMEAL

½ CUP SUGAR

2 STICKS COLD BUTTER, CUBED

½ CUP COLD WATER IN A SPRAY BOTTLE

2 TART APPLES, PEELED, CORED, THINLY SLICED

3 TABLESPOONS CIDER VINEGAR

¼ TEASPOON GROUND NUTMEG

¼ TEASPOON GROUND MACE

2 TABLESPOONS BUTTER

½ CUP SHREDDED SHARP CHEDDAR CHEESE

1 TEASPOON FLOUR

1 EGG WHITE

IRISH SODA BREAD

Irish Soda Bread

YIELDS 1 LOAF

1. Place a rack in the upper third of the oven and preheat to 400°F. Place a Dutch oven on the rack. Whisk together the flours, sugar, baking soda, cream of tartar, and salt. Cut 2 tablespoons of the butter into small bits and use forks or a pastry knife to work the butter into the flour mixture until it's crumbly and coarse.

2. Add the buttermilk and stir with a fork until the dough has just come together. Sprinkle some flour onto a surface and knead the dough until everything sticks together and it is still bumpy.

3. Pat the dough into a circle the size of your pan and no more than 2" thick. Cut an *X* into the top of the dough.

4. Place the dough in the Dutch oven, cover, and bake for 20 minutes. Bake, uncovered, for another 20–25 minutes. Rub the remaining butter on top of the crust and let the loaf sit for 30 minutes or until it has cooled.

3 CUPS ALL-PURPOSE FLOUR

1 CUP CAKE FLOUR

2 TABLESPOONS SUGAR

1½ TEASPOONS BAKING SODA

1½ TEASPOONS CREAM OF TARTAR

2 TEASPOONS SALT

3 TABLESPOONS BUTTER, SOFTENED

1½ CUPS BUTTERMILK

Upside-Down Apple Pie

YIELDS 8 SERVINGS

1. Add the flour, sugar, and salt to a food processor. Pulse a few times. Add the cold butter and pulse till it resembles coarse cornmeal. Pour the mixture into a bowl. Stir in the egg until chunks form. If necessary, add a little cold water to get this consistency. Press the chunks together into a disk and wrap in plastic wrap. Refrigerate for at least 1 hour.

2. Place a rack in the middle of the oven and preheat to 375°F. Place a skillet over medium heat. Add the butter and when melted add the sugar. Cook for 5 minutes. Stir in the spices and cook for 1 minute more. Turn off the heat.

3. Layer the apple slices around the outside of the pan so the tips are touching the skillet wall and the thin edge of each slice is under the thicker edge of the slice next to it. Fill in the center with apple slices. Cook over high heat for 12 minutes or until the caramel mixture is very dark and the apples have soaked up most of it. Tilt the pan to cover the apple slices with juice. Cook for 5 minutes. Turn off the heat.

4. Meanwhile, roll the dough between 2 sheets of parchment paper into a 14" circle. Place the dough on the skillet. Tuck the dough edges under so they touch the skillet but are not visible. Cut four 1" slits in the center of the pie.

5. Bake for 20–25 minutes, or until the crust is golden brown. Let cool for 20 minutes. Loosen the edges of the crust with a knife. Place a plate on top of the skillet and invert. Scrape out any apples that stick and rearrange them on top.

2¼ CUPS ALL-PURPOSE FLOUR

¼ CUP CONFECTIONERS' SUGAR

¾ TEASPOON SALT

6 TABLESPOONS BUTTER, COLD AND CUBED

1 EGG, LIGHTLY BEATEN

2 TABLESPOONS COLD WATER (IF NEEDED)

6 TABLESPOONS BUTTER

⅔ CUP GRANULATED SUGAR

¼ TEASPOON NUTMEG

1 TEASPOON CINNAMON

½ TEASPOON GROUND CARDAMOM

3 POUNDS FUJI OR GRANNY SMITH APPLES, CORED, PEELED, SLICED

Fried Malassadas

YIELDS 5 DOZEN MALASSADAS

1. Place the yeast, ⅓ cup warm water, and 1 teaspoon sugar in a bowl and let the yeast dissolve and become frothy. Stir the flour, salt, and ⅓ cup sugar in a large bowl. Mix the cream and 1⅓ cups water in a small bowl. Add to the flour mixture.

2. Stir the butter and eggs into the flour mixture. Add the yeast mixture and mix until the dough is soft and cannot be stirred. Knead lightly on a surface until smooth.

3. Place 1 teaspoon oil into a large clean bowl. Add the ball of dough and turn until coated. Cover the bowl with a towel and place in a warm, draft-free area for 1–2 hours or until doubled. Punch down and divide into 4 even balls. Use your hands to roll the 4 portions into tubes.

4. Place a chicken fryer over medium-high heat. Add the oil. Once it's hot, pinch off portions of dough that are 2" square. Cook on each side for 1–2 minutes until they're lightly golden brown and soft but not raw in the middle. Drain on a wire rack over paper towels and sprinkle with sugar. Serve hot or warm.

1 PACKAGE FAST-ACTING YEAST

1⅔ CUPS WARM WATER

1 TEASPOON PLUS ⅓ CUP SUGAR

6–7 CUPS FLOUR

1 TEASPOON SALT

1⅓ CUPS CREAM OR MILK

⅓ CUP MELTED BUTTER

8 EGGS, BEATEN

1 QUART VEGETABLE OIL

Chocolate Chip Skillet Cookie

YIELDS 2 SKILLET-SIZED COOKIES

1. Preheat oven to 350°F.

2. Combine the flour, baking soda, and salt in a bowl.

3. Use the paddle attachment of a stand mixer, or a use a hand-held mixer, to cream ¾ cup butter and sugars until they're light and fluffy. Add the egg and vanilla and blend on low until combined. Add the flour mixture and beat on low until it is just combined. Stir in the chocolate chips by hand.

4. Grease a 4"–6" skillet with 1 teaspoon of butter. Divide the dough in half. Transfer half of the dough to the skillet and press to flatten evenly over the bottom of the skillet. Bake for 30 minutes, or until the edges are brown and the top is golden. Repeat with the other half of the dough.

5. Leave in the pan and rest on a wire rack for 10 minutes to cool. Cut and serve.

2 CUPS ALL-PURPOSE FLOUR

1 TEASPOON BAKING SODA

½ TEASPOON SALT

¾ CUP PLUS 1 TEASPOON UNSALTED BUTTER, SOFTENED

½ CUP SUGAR

¾ CUP PACKED BROWN SUGAR

1 EGG

2 TEASPOONS VANILLA EXTRACT

1½ CUPS CHOCOLATE CHIPS

CHOCOLATE CHIP SKILLET COOKIE

U.S./Metric Conversion Chart

VOLUME CONVERSIONS

U.S. Volume Measure	Metric Equivalent
⅛ teaspoon	0.5 milliliter
¼ teaspoon	1 milliliter
½ teaspoon	2 milliliters
1 teaspoon	5 milliliters
½ tablespoon	7 milliliters
1 tablespoon (3 teaspoons)	15 milliliters
2 tablespoons (1 fluid ounce)	30 milliliters
¼ cup (4 tablespoons)	60 milliliters
⅓ cup	90 milliliters
½ cup (4 fluid ounces)	125 milliliters
⅔ cup	160 milliliters
¾ cup (6 fluid ounces)	180 milliliters
1 cup (16 tablespoons)	250 milliliters
1 pint (2 cups)	500 milliliters
1 quart (4 cups)	1 liter (about)

WEIGHT CONVERSIONS

U.S. Weight Measure	Metric Equivalent
½ ounce	15 grams
1 ounce	30 grams
2 ounces	60 grams
3 ounces	85 grams
¼ pound (4 ounces)	115 grams
½ pound (8 ounces)	225 grams
¾ pound (12 ounces)	340 grams
1 pound (16 ounces)	454 grams

OVEN TEMPERATURE CONVERSIONS

Degrees Fahrenheit	Degrees Celsius
200 degrees F	95 degrees C
250 degrees F	120 degrees C
275 degrees F	135 degrees C
300 degrees F	150 degrees C
325 degrees F	160 degrees C
350 degrees F	180 degrees C
375 degrees F	190 degrees C
400 degrees F	205 degrees C
425 degrees F	220 degrees C
450 degrees F	230 degrees C

BAKING PAN SIZES

American	Metric
8 × 1½ inch round baking pan	20 × 4 cm cake tin
9 × 1½ inch round baking pan	23 × 3.5 cm cake tin
11 × 7 × 1½ inch baking pan	28 × 18 × 4 cm baking tin
13 × 9 × 2 inch baking pan	30 × 20 × 5 cm baking tin
2 quart rectangular baking dish	30 × 20 × 3 cm baking tin
15 × 10 × 2 inch baking pan	30 × 25 × 2 cm baking tin (Swiss roll tin)
9 inch pie plate	22 × 4 or 23 × 4 cm pie plate
7 or 8 inch springform pan	18 or 20 cm springform or loose bottom cake tin
9 × 5 × 3 inch loaf pan	23 × 13 × 7 cm or 2 lb narrow loaf or pate tin
1½ quart casserole	1.5 liter casserole
2 quart casserole	2 liter casserole

Index